Ryan
CHAMBERLIN

Frank
VISCUSO

The
MENTOR

The Dream...The Struggle...The Prize

May the Math

Burn The Boats

**Residual
PUBLISHING**

www.residualpublishing.com

Copyright © 2012 by Ryan Chamberlin and Frank Viscuso
Published by Residual Publishing a subdivision of STM Publication
143 NW Perkins Place
Lake City, FL 32055
Co-published by Now You Know Press

ISBN 978-0-9797553-6-1

Library of Congress Cataloging-in-Publication Data

Cover design: Remnant Graphic Design

The Mentor
Success-- Network Marketing-- Personal Growth. 1. Title – Fiction

www.ryanchamberlin.com
www.commonvalor.com

Printed in the United States of America

10 9 8 7 6 5 4 3 2 1

CONTENTS

Meet the Authors

RYAN CHAMBERLIN is a network marketing expert, a speaker, author, consultant, and mentor. In addition to building some of the largest teams in the industry, he is also known for his development of systems, and cutting-edge training techniques, which have been adopted by thousands. These practices continue to produce hundreds of millions of dollars in sales. Now, in his late thirties, Ryan is one of the most sought-after speakers and motivators in the industry. He spends the majority of his time mentoring and consulting high performers and leaders in areas of personal and professional development. His first book, *Now You Know! Why some succeed and others fail using the same system*, reveals the seven laws of sales, which are the foundation for the teachings described in *the Mentor*. Ryan lives in Belleview, Florida, with his wife, Jenny, and their four boys—Alexander, Andrew, Anthony, and Avery.

FRANK VISCUSO is a speaker, entrepreneur, fire chief and author of three books including the best-selling *Fireground Operational Guides*. He was introduced to network marketing when he was twenty-five years old. After struggling early on, Frank analyzed, reviewed and applied the industry's top leaders' principles to his business. From there, he developed and lead one of the largest teams in the Northeastern United States. Frank is an advocate for network marketing and personal growth, with an undying passion for teaching and motivating others. He credits the industry for empowering him with the necessary skills he needed to succeed as a leader, team builder, and trainer, both in and out of the direct selling industry. Frank resides in Toms River, New Jersey, with his wife Laura, and their three boys – Thomas, Frankie and Nicholas.

6

Acknowledgements

I WOULD LIKE TO thank true friends; those who remain, no matter what path life takes you down. A special thanks to my co-writer, Frank Viscuso, and his wife, Laura, for their countless hours invested into this project...hashing and re-hashing the content. To my wife, partner, and best friend, Jenny; thank you for your continual contribution into our marriage, family, and business.

Ryan Chamberlin

I WOULD LIKE TO thank my friends, Steve Moss, Caleb and Gina Edmond, Jeff and Dina Wittner, Scott and Brooke Carrell, Michael Credico, Vijay Bharatiya, Manish Ramani, and James Leonhardt for supporting this book. To the thousands of networkers I have met, shared ideas with, and learned from throughout the years, you are among the finest people I have ever known. I encourage all of you to continue to do your part in making this a better world. A special thank you is extended to Ryan and Jenny Chamberlin, a dynamic couple my wife and I treasure as friends. Most of all, to my beautiful wife and best friend, Laura; you are truly an amazing wife and mother. Thank you for partnering with me on life's journey.

Frank Viscuso

Dedication

The MENTOR *is dedicated to those whose dreams have brought on struggles, and whose persistence will guarantee their prize.*

Ryan Chamberlin
Frank Viscuso

Opportunity Knocks

IT WAS STILL RAINING in Northern New Jersey when Michael, and his three buddies, left the hotel that evening. Not as heavy as before. It was soft and warm; as if the last drops would dissipate into the ground before the boys reached the car.

"Have you ever walked into a movie theater when it's raining, only to come out two hours later and find it sunny?" Dean asked.

"Yeah," Billy replied with a chuckle and a smirk, "That's weird."

Michael found it odd that Dean and Billy rarely talked about things that he found important. He almost felt as if the two shared some sort of secret, perhaps one that gave them an advantage in life that he wasn't fortunate enough to have. This would explain why the presentation they had all just seen didn't excite either of them, as much as it did him.

Dean was the son of a prestigious bank vice-president. Even as a teenager, he was never without the coolest gadgets and most expensive toys. At thirty, he was more established than the others were. He no longer had to rent a house, but rather owned a home, in a nice neighborhood, and drove a gorgeous black Audi. Dean was on the fast track to success. He was following in his father's footsteps and working at the same branch; already in line to be the next junior VP.

The friends took their usual seats in Dean's luxury car, as the conversation continued without purpose. Billy jumped in the passenger seat, while Michael and Tom took their places in the back.

"Drop me off first so I can catch the end of the game." Billy directed.

His request didn't surprise Michael or the others. Billy worked in construction. He was a star athlete back in high school where he earned nine Varsity letters. Baseball was his main sport, and although his high school heroics took place twelve years ago, he still acted as if he was the talk of the town. The truth; however, was that no one outside of the four of them even remembered Billy's athletic accomplishments. Twelve years is a long time, and in that timeframe, many things have changed, except for Billy, of course. Whether or not he had a good day was usually determined by the outcome of the Yankees game the day before. His priorities were definitely jumbled. Perhaps that was one of the reasons why he had worked for five different contractors over the past year, unable to secure a steady job.

Although they had been friends since high school, Billy had a way of getting on Michael's nerves. Maybe it was the way he made excuses for the prosperity and achievements of others. Billy would often say things like, *"he got lucky,"* or *"he only has money because his grandparents left it to him."* Even if those reasons were valid, it was frustrating for Michael to hear Billy make excuses every time they talked about success. Michael believed that hard work had to come into the equation somewhere. Sadly, it wasn't in Billy's nature to give someone that much credit. He'd rather just chalk it up as luck.

Michael couldn't remember the last time the two engaged in conversation without it becoming heated. Billy didn't use logic to explain his point of view, he used VOLUME. If raising his voice didn't work, he would try to win arguments by flashing his signature smirk and rolling his eyes at the opposing party. This is why Michael preferred to sit *behind* Billy in the car.

As they drove out of the hotel parking lot, Michael took it upon himself to initiate a conversation on what they had just seen. He looked at his buddy, who was sitting next to him, "So, what do you think, Tom?"

Tom was the quiet one. He was a thin accountant; who has skills with numbers, but often lacks the ability to make eye contact with strangers. "I don't know. Everything the guy said made sense. But I don't know anyone who would be interested in something like that."

A peculiar response, Michael thought. "You don't know *anybody* who would be interested in making more money?" he asked.

As expected, Billy jumped in, "You're not really considering doing it, are you Michael?"

"We came here to look at a way to make more money, didn't we?" Michael asked. "I mean, I'm barely getting ahead, you're no better off than I am, and Tom has a second child on the way."

Billy rolled down his window, which caused some rain to enter the car and land on Michael's face. He couldn't help but to feel as if that was his friend's intention. "I came because it was an excuse to have dinner and a couple drinks with you guys," Billy said, justifying himself. "Now that I've seen the business, we can say we're not interested, and move on."

Considering the facts that Michael and Tom don't drink, and dinner was a slice of pizza in Hoboken, it was another one of Billy's senseless responses.

Michael and the others were silent. Billy rested his arm on the door, leaned his head back and completed his thought with, "Nobody makes money in these 'get-rich-quick-schemes'."

"The guy at the hotel seemed to be doing well," Michael replied nonchalantly.

"Hey, if you want to do it, then do it." Billy said, raising his voice with each word. He turned his head enough so that Michael could see his smirk. "Let me know when you make your first million."

"Alright Billy, that's enough," Dean jumped in. He was usually the referee between the two.

The conversation was held to a minimum as Dean dropped both Billy and Tom off at their apartments. Once the two of them were alone, Dean and Michael had the chance to talk openly. Dean thought this would be a great time to warn Michael.

"You have to be careful when you join one of these pyramids."

"The guy said it's not a pyramid," Michael said.

"I know what he said, but people relate it to one, and it's your reputation that'll be on the line. If you make promises and don't deliver, you'll make a fool of yourself."

"I'm not making any promises, I just think that if all four of us do it, we can make it work," Michael explained.

"Tom would never do it," Dean assured. "His wife makes the decisions in their house. He doesn't even dress himself. And you can forget Billy. He'll sign up when the shortstop for the Yankees does."

"What about you?" Michael asked. He was certain that with Dean's credibility, if he signed up, the others would follow.

"Me?" Dean said, with a crooked smile. "I'd be crazy to get involved with a network marketing company. I can't risk all that I've worked for."

Risk what HE worked for? Michael thought. *Who is he kidding?* Michael knew Dean's early advancement was a result of his father's influence. He wasn't foolish enough to think otherwise. Knowing the facts didn't change the reality that Michael was barely keeping his own head above water. Ever since Michael began working as a manual laborer and machine operator at a distribution warehouse in Jersey City, he had been living on a tight budget. His wife, Kristen, worked as a grammar school teacher. The couple was living in a small home in northern New Jersey, and raising their eight-month-old son. Michael couldn't remember the last time they put money in their savings account. He wasn't even sure if they still had one.

Walking towards his house, Michael turned and watched Dean's Audi fade from sight. He was happy that his friend was financially secure, but the truth was, he was also envious. It was easy for Dean to give Michael advice on what he should and shouldn't do, because Dean had help from his father along the way. Michael wasn't as fortunate. It caused him to wonder, perhaps for the first time ever, if he was taking advice from the right person.

"Who am I listening to?" he whispered.

It was a question worth asking.

Lost Dreams

KRISTEN DIDN'T COME to the door to greet Michael when he entered the house. In the past, she always provided a refreshing welcome, but the financial stress they were both under had been taking its toll on them for quite some time. Kristen was a beautiful woman with a slender body, long blonde wavy hair, and a knack for dressing. One would naturally assume she shopped at the finest designer boutiques in New York City. The reality was quite the opposite, however. The couple operated on such a tight budget she hadn't bought herself a nice dress in years. Just the idea of walking into an expensive store seemed absurd considering their current struggles.

One night, Michael was sitting in the living room, secretly watching his wife, who was in the kitchen browsing through a catalog. He observed her staring at a particular item for quite a while, when she took her pen and circled it. Around and around he saw the pen go.

A few moments passed before she sighed heavily, ripped out the page, crumbled it up, and threw it in the trashcan.

Michael found her behavior unusual, so later that evening he retrieved the paper and flattened it out.

His heart sank when he realized it was a picture of the designer Coach bag she had always wanted. Shame and guilt overcame him as the weight of the matter set in. He knew that she thought even *dreaming* of such a non-essential purchase was ridiculous.

He never said a word about the photo. The grave financial reality they were faced with bothered Michael immensely.

When they first met, Kristen rarely complained about anything. Even during their first years of marriage, no matter how bad a day she had, she never failed to show her smile when Michael came home. The gesture was something that Michael was always grateful for. Lately, he had become so preoccupied by the demands of daily life, that he was completely unaware that he hadn't verbalized his appreciation in a long time. A very long time. Perhaps that was one of the reasons why their relationship seemed different—strained—even though there was still much love between the two of them.

Michael entered his house and closed the door behind him. He walked into the living room where Kristen was watching television. She half-stood and he half-leaned over to meet for a brief kiss. "How's Dylan?" he asked.

"He's great, sound asleep. He tried applesauce tonight for the first time. He loved it."

Michael smiled, but didn't respond.

Kristen continued, "How did it go?"

"It was okay," he said, with a disappointing tone.

"Just okay? You were excited before you left. What happened?" Kristen paused, "Let me guess. They want you to spend money and more time away from home, right?"

The comment didn't come as a surprise to Michael. When Kristen was younger, she was very athletic and participated in a variety of sports. Her favorite was soccer. She excelled at the game from the initial moment she stepped on the field. When she was twelve-years-old, her coach put her in as the goalkeeper for the first game of the season. Although this was the first time she tried out for the sport, her athleticism caused the coach to think she would be the person for the job. He made the right call. Kristen made nine saves during the game and was the team standout. Here was the problem. The game ended in a zero-zero tie. They needed a striker, a girl who could put the ball in the net. On the following weekend, the coach put another girl in as the goalkeeper and brought Kristen up to the front of the field for the game. He wanted to utilize her speed and ability to run with the ball. She scored three goals and her team won 3-2. Even though it was only the second game she had ever played, she was named team captain.

Most girls her age would be thrilled to have this kind of success early on, but Kristen's experience was overshadowed by the fact that her father was never there to see her play. He was out working his second job. Kristen's father was an electrician. He worked long hours as it was, but was never able to land the union job that he thought was the answer to his financial challenges. When he was offered a job driving a delivery truck on weekends, he reluctantly took it. He promised his daughter it was going to be temporary. It wasn't. He fell into the trap of trading his time for dollars—a trap he never found a way out of.

To this day, Kristen's not even sure if her father knew she was the team captain and leading scorer. He again promised that after the season, he would never miss another game. Instead, he took a third job and went from missing her games to missing more significant events like birthdays, holidays, and family get-togethers. Before she turned fifteen, her parents were divorced, with her mother receiving sole custody. Kristen could count on one hand how many times she has seen her father since. She always blamed the time her father spent away from the family for the breakup of her parent's marriage.

Michael understood where his wife was coming from, so he decided to tread lightly. Still, he wanted to discuss what he had just seen because he valued her opinion.

"Everything the speaker said made sense, but I don't know anyone who would be interested in doing it," Michael explained. It didn't take long for him to realize those were Tom's words, not his own. He corrected himself, "I mean, maybe some people would be interested, just not *my* friends."

Kristen could tell Michael was upset. She knew he was hoping this was going to turn out to be something good for their family, and a part of her hoped it would be as well. Out of her mouth came the words, "Whatever you decide to do, you know I support you." Deep down inside, both their stomach's churned. Michael was already working 60 hours a week. He didn't have any more time to spend away from home and his family. More than anything, she didn't want her marriage to end the way her parents' marriage did.

"I know you do," he said with a tender smile.

There was a time when Michael thought he was going to accomplish big things. Huge things! That was many years ago. Perhaps, if he had been presented with this opportunity five years earlier, he would have jumped on board and done something with it, but now he questioned whether or not he still had that spark inside of him.

After Kristen went to bed, and the house was quiet, Michael sat in the dark. With just the glow of television keeping him company, he wondered where his dreams had gone.

3

Make a Move

IT WAS TWO O'CLOCK in the morning. Michael couldn't sleep. He was lying in bed looking up at the ceiling and wondering; *where did I go wrong?* He was thirty-years-old and felt like a complete failure. Working hard was never a problem, but Michael had reached the point where he was beginning to realize that hard work wasn't enough.

He had been overwhelmed with paying the bills on time and keeping up with the mortgage. It seemed every day there was another late notice in the mailbox. His credit was destroyed. Both he and Kristen were finding it more and more difficult to live on their stagnant salaries, especially with the rising cost of food, childcare, property taxes, and health insurance. Adding to their stress was a recent medical bill resulting from their baby's unexpected five-day stay in the hospital. The baby had a severe reaction to amoxicillin that caused several days of high fever, coupled with a full body rash and swelling. The doctors originally thought the baby had contracted a rare virus or disease. However, on the fourth day, without explanation, the symptoms began to reverse. The doctors told Michael and Kristen they would have to wait it out. It was suggested they go home and return to the hospital if the symptoms began to intensify again. This didn't make sense to Michael and quite frankly scared him and Kristen, so they requested one more day of observation and care by the medical staff.

During the fifth day, the baby's symptoms continued to regress. Since the doctors didn't actually provide "treatment" on that day, the insurance company decided not to cover the expenses. Just occupying a room, and having the nurses visit several times to check the baby's vitals and temperature resulted in a thousand dollar bill that Michael had to pay out of pocket. He was in a losing battle with the claim's department over the incident. To make matters worse, a buddy pointed out that his car needed two new front tires. He simply couldn't catch a break! The thought of money, or lack thereof, was on his mind day in and day out.

One evening, a few weeks later, he was sitting on the couch reading the paper, when he began experiencing tightness in his chest and labored breathing. *This can't be a heart attack*, he told himself. A few minutes later, Kristen found him on his knees in the bathroom.

"Michael!" She screamed.

"I'm okay," he assured. "I just need to catch my breath."

They rushed to the local hospital, praying that Michael wasn't suffering a fate similar to his father, Tim, who died suddenly at the age of fifty-four.

Shortly after they arrived at St. Michaels' Medical Center, the feeling subsided. The doctor explained that Michael had just experienced a panic attack. The stress was beginning to take its toll. The doctor ordered well-needed rest, but Michael couldn't afford to miss work. That uneasy, chest gripping feeling seemed to have become a part of his existence.

For more than a year, Michael felt as if he was running up a downward moving escalator. He had been praying for an answer to his financial challenges for a long time. While staring up at the ceiling of his bedroom, he thought of the joke the speaker told at the meeting. It was about a man who was stranded on his rooftop after a flash flood. The man prayed for God to save him. While sitting on his roof, the stranded man turned down help from rescuers on a boat and a helicopter. Both times he yelled out to his would-be rescuers, "God will save me!" After losing his life to the rising floodwaters he came face to face with God and asked, "Why didn't you save me?" Only to have God reply, "I tried twice. I sent you a boat and a helicopter."

Is this opportunity the answer to my prayers? As he pondered the question, the rain began to fall hard again. Unable to remember if he had closed the downstairs windows, he quietly rose from bed and walked through the house to inspect. In the living room, he noticed the drapes moving from the howling breeze. He closed the window and realized the breeze had knocked over one a family portrait. Michael picked up the photo. It was a picture of his father when he was in his early forties.

Looking at the picture caused moments from his childhood to flash through his mind. He thought about visiting his father at the firehouse where he worked. He remembered how important he felt walking into the station and having his dad introduce him to the other firefighters. The guys went out of their way to show Michael the equipment and let him sit on the Engine. For a ten-year-old boy, a private tour of a fire station was as good as it gets.

Michael also thought about the words of encouragement that his father gave him before his wrestling matches in high school. "He puts his pants on one leg at a time, just like you do," his father used to say about his opponents. Michael remembered how hesitant he was to ask his high school crush to his senior prom. His father nudged him to just pick up the phone and make the call. She said yes. That was another great memory of the way Michael's father reassured him when he needed it the most. The memories ran through his mind like a movie in fast forward. Quick flashes, until Michael began to recall the events that occurred four years earlier, when his father passed away. Michael and Kristen were both twenty-six years old at the time. They had just signed the lease and moved into their home. It was an exciting time for them, but a chaotic one. Their living room was full of boxes and a single mattress that sat on the floor, next to a second-hand couch and coffee table. The couple was rummaging through the contents of one of the boxes when the phone rang.

"Our first phone call," Kristen said, as she hurried to answer it.

"I bet it's a telemarketer," Michael laughed.

Kristen picked up the phone and greeted the caller with a cheerful, "Hello, this is the Harper residence." They both chuckled, but Kristen's smile quickly faded. "Yes, he's here. Is everything okay?"

Michael's body went numb. Somehow, he knew.

Two days later, he was wearing a suit and shaking hands with people he hadn't seen in years; the same people he would only see at weddings... and funerals.

Michael reminisced, in vivid detail, walking out onto the front porch at Mulligan's Funeral Parlor for a much needed moment by himself. He had been speaking with family and friends about his father for nearly two hours and needed to step away to take a breath and gather his composure. His father was his rock for as long as he could remember. Whenever Michael had a problem, his father was always there for him. He was a man of few words, but the words he used mattered. Accepting the fact that he was gone was not easy for Michael. It all happened so quickly that he didn't even have a chance to properly mourn his loss. As he stood on the porch, leaning on the railing and watching cars pass, a man walked up, stood beside him and started talking.

"I grew up with your father. He was an honest man and a good friend. There aren't many people like him left in this world," the man said.

"Thank you. That's very kind." Michael replied.

"I doubt you remember me. You were only about ten the last time I saw you. My name is Blake Easton."

Michael knew the name. Everyone from the neighborhood Michael grew up in knew the name. Blake Easton was somewhat of a legend. He was a high school dropout who somehow became a multi-millionaire. Certainly, there was more to this "rags-to-riches" story, but Michael didn't know the details. What he did know was that Blake Easton was an entrepreneur, and one of the nicest guys around. He had heard stories from his father about how Blake donated a lot of time and money to charitable causes such as church renovations and the financing of homeless shelters. For Michael, the story that stood out the most was the one where when the millionaire filled up a moving truck with brand new toys and brought them to an orphanage for the holidays. The rumor was that Blake wanted to remain anonymous, but a reporter who got wind of the story tracked the presents back to a local toy store and found an employee who leaked the millionaire's name.

Michael was always impressed by what he knew of Blake and his story. He was also aware that his father vaguely knew the millionaire, but he didn't expect to meet him at his father's wake. He turned to look at the millionaire.

Blake was about 5' 9" with wild, but slightly tamed dark hair. He was obviously well-dressed, but looked more like a surfer than a businessman. He appeared to be much younger than Michael's father was. Maybe it was his perfect tan, not like the one a person gets from a tanning salon or a bottle. It was more like one you'd see on someone who just came back from two weeks on an island in the Caribbean. If not the tan, perhaps it was the absence of gray hair that made Blake look ten years younger. Whatever the reason, none of that mattered right now. They shook hands.

"It's nice to meet you Mr. Easton. I heard stories about you from my father."

"Call me Blake. And I meant what I said about your father. He was exceptional."

"That means a lot to me."

"Son, if there is anything I can ever do for you, don't hesitate to call." Blake handed Michael his business card. "My cell number is on the back."

"Thank you."

"I'm serious," Blake stressed, "anything."

"Thank you, and thank you for coming."

"He'll be missed," Blake assured.

They shook hands again. This time Blake kept a firm grip for a moment and looked Michael in the eyes as if he was putting an exclamation point on the conversation. After the millionaire released his grip and walked off the porch, Michael glanced at the business card. It was a simple card that read '*Blake Easton, entrepreneur*' with a phone number on the bottom. Michael placed the millionaire's business card in his wallet and returned into the funeral parlor.

Although the encounter Michael had with Blake at the funeral parlor four years earlier was brief, it was the only one that evening which he remembered with such vivid detail. He wasn't quite sure why he thought of that interaction now, but the photo he clutched in his hands, was a reminder of the pain Michael felt the day he lost his father. The picture he was holding showed the face of a man who seemed to have his whole life ahead of him. *What if he made different choices?* Michael thought. *He lived with integrity and he cared about others, but he struggled with finances his whole life, just like I am now. What if he made different choices?*

As he sat on the couch with the photo in his hands, for the first time, he did more than just look at the picture. This time, he studied it. His father looked happy, but worn. He was smiling, but only because the photo was being taken. Just a few of the hairs on top of his head held their original color. He seemed to be talking to Michael through the photo, his wrinkled eyes saying, *Make your move son. Don't end up living with regret. Learn from my mistakes. The opportunity you have your hands on was not put in front of you by accident. There are no accidents. Everything happens for a reason.*

What if it works and I don't do it? Michael said—thinking about how his life could change if he took advantage of the opportunity that was just presented to him. He wondered if his son would be looking at a similar photo of him someday, years from now, thinking the same thoughts he was thinking. Michael wiped away a tear that was clinging to his chin, and returned to bed.

Too Good to Be True

MICHAEL STEPPED OUT of the shower and was greeted by a familiar aroma that filled the house. He loved Kristen's egg-white omelet and home fries. He hurried to put his jeans and t-shirt on so he could enjoy a good breakfast and spend a few minutes with his family. The couple would have to leave for work soon. As he walked towards the bedroom door, he noticed the computer was on. Kristen must have been checking her email. Michael was still distracted by Billy's comment from the night before...nobody makes money in network marketing. *That can't be true,* he thought.

The Internet is not the most reliable place to seek answers. The fact is, anybody can post their comments on a webpage and try to pass themselves off as an expert. Many of these so-called experts don't even leave their name. Even though Michael was aware of this fact, it didn't stop him from sitting down and typing a question into Google's search box. "Does anyone make money in network marketing?" Michael scrolled down the list of results and clicked on a link.

The article, printed in *Success from Home* magazine, talked about the millions of Americans that were taking advantage of this multi-billion dollar industry. The author mentioned Warren Buffet, one of the wealthiest men in the world, and arguably the most successful investor who ever lived, was a supporter of network marketing. So much so, it mentioned that he invested in, and owned several multi-level marketing companies. There were also endorsements from several other business experts including Robert Kiyosaki, bestselling author of the *Rich Dad* book series and billionaire, Donald Trump. The article was very supportive of the industry. There was one fact in particular that really captured Michael's attention. Millions of people worldwide were using the network marketing industry to develop secondary, and even primary incomes. It also stated that more people have become millionaires from network marketing and direct selling than from any other business model.

Could this be true? Michael wondered. *If so, how could anyone think that money can't be made in these things?*

He continued to read... During the last recession, the network marketing industry had grown by 77% worldwide. That was a staggering number considering many well-known corporations had struggled and failed during that same timeframe. This brought light to another truth. The industry helped protect people from looming financial catastrophes. If a person develops a team in several regions, states and even countries, they would better protect themselves from uncontrollable factors that could take down a local business. For instance, natural disasters, demographics or economic challenges. Near the end of the article, it was mentioned how many people dismiss network marketing companies as "get-rich-quick" schemes. Michael found this interesting since that was exactly what Billy said in the car - the night before. However, the article did stress the legitimacy of the industry. Clearly, those who work their businesses hard are often pleased with the results.

"It's obviously not a 'get-rich-quick' scheme," Michael said, before silently completing his thought, *but it sure looks like people are getting rich doing it.*

The article left Michael with more questions than answers. He wondered about its validity, but certainly, the publication appeared much more credible than his friend Billy's uneducated opinion. He knew that he would have to do more research and ask many more questions, but who could he ask? Perhaps, Blake Easton could provide some insight. Maybe that was why he subconsciously recalled their meeting four years earlier. Michael contemplated that possibility as he logged off and made his way downstairs.

Kristen was at the stove. The baby was in his highchair, smiling and being his usual playful self.

"Smells terrific," Michael complimented, "Can I help with anything?"

"No thanks. Breakfast is ready. Have a seat."

Michael took his place at the table and started to play with the baby. Kristen could see the tiredness in her husband's eyes, "I take it you didn't sleep well?"

"No, but I'll make up for it tonight."

Scattered on the table were about a dozen test papers that Kristen did not have a chance to review and grade the night before. Michael knew his wife was worn down physically and emotionally from balancing work, the baby, and home. She didn't complain about working hard. Neither of them did. Hard work was not the problem. Not seeing the finish line was.

Kristen brought two plates to the table and sat to join Michael for breakfast. She immediately turned her attention to the papers, leaving Michael to think back when things were more simple.

Two of the most appealing qualities Michael found in Kristen when they first met were her optimism and sense of humor. The first time he experienced her refreshing disposition was back when they first started dating. He was driving her home one night after a romantic dinner. In an attempt to extend the date by a few more minutes, he began driving slowly down her street—so slow, that when a black cat crossed in front of their car, neither could miss seeing it. Knowing this is considered a sign of bad luck, his immediate thought was *that's not good*, but before he could open his mouth Kristen said, "It was navy blue."

They laughed heartily for almost a minute. She was definitely an optimist. At least, she used to be. Michael, on the other hand, always considered himself a realist, but the way the last few years had gone, he was beginning to think that maybe he was becoming a pessimist. After all, it's a fine line to walk—realist to pessimist. He wanted to change his outlook and his circumstances .He was finally beginning to realize that for things to change, he would have to change first.

Kristen continued to grade her papers, "Do you have a few dollars for the dry cleaning?" she asked.

Michael reached into his back pocket and pulled out his worn leather wallet. It was overstuffed with things that didn't need to be there, definitely a habit he inherited from his father. He looked in the money compartment and noticed that he only had one twenty-dollar bill and a couple of singles.

"Is twenty enough?"

"That should be fine."

Michael passed the wrinkled twenty-dollar bill across the table. He folded his wallet. Before returning it to his pocket, a thought hit him. He reopened the wallet and squeezed his pointer finger into the hidden compartment behind his license. He could feel a stiff piece of paper inside. He wiggled his finger in a way that revealed enough of the item that he could grab one corner and pull it out. Surprisingly, there it was. Blake Easton's card—and his cell number, although faint, it was still legible.

Momentarily, he looked at his wife and then at his baby. He reminisced about how wonderful it is to watch Kristen play with Dylan. He visualized the baby laughing, the way only an eight-month old can, and like he did so often. They're so beautiful and happy together, but it's so hard to watch them during those moments that should be carefree. The heavy burden of money put a damper on those special times—all the time.

Michael held the card in his hand for what seemed like an eternity. He contemplated the countless times he asked his broke friends for advice, but never called someone who truly understood business. Maybe this was a sign.

"Do you remember Blake Easton?" he asked. Kristen lifted her head and gave a quizzical look. "He's the millionaire that grew up with my father. The one who gave me his card at dad's funeral?"

"Oh, yes," Kristen replied, returning her attention to the papers.

"I'm going to call him today."

Kristen redirected her attention back to Michael, "What for?"

He took a moment to choose the proper words, "My whole life I've been waiting for a sign. Something to tell me what I'm supposed to be doing. That sign never came. I can't sit and wait anymore. This man is the most successful person I know, well—kind of know. For some reason, I thought of him last night and it got me thinking. If he would be willing to give me advice, I'd be crazy not to take advantage of that opportunity."

"What are you going to ask him about?"

"I'm not exactly sure." Michael replied with raised eyebrows. "I guess I just want to get his opinion on a number of things. One of them being the business I just looked at, and maybe some guidance about finances and success, in general. It couldn't hurt, right?"

"I suppose not. I think it's a good idea," she agreed, with a half-approving smile.

Michael wasn't convinced that his wife did agree. After breakfast, he donned his work shirt and left the house. Putting that shirt on was always the last thing Michael did before leaving the house. It was an unappealing, faded blue, button down shirt with his name written on a patch that sat crooked and to the left, on his chest. For Michael, the shirt was a reminder of his failures. It represented the inadequate income and strained lifestyle that his family had become accustomed to. Regardless of his dejected feelings about the shirt and his job, Michael was a hard worker. He never let his grim feelings keep him from doing what he felt he needed to do to provide for his family.

One Thousand Dollars

I HATE TRAFFIC.

Michael's right foot moved back and forth from the gas pedal to the brake pedal. It was another daily ritual—*traffic*—forty minutes of stop and go, five days a week, fifty weeks a year. Making matters worse was the fact that Kristen was also sitting in traffic. She would typically leave the house twenty minutes after he did and head in a different direction. Her commute to work began by taking Dylan to daycare. After a tearful goodbye, Kristen would reluctantly head to work. He and Kristen were disheartened with their necessity for daycare. On his way to work, Michael thought about how great it would be if he made enough money so Kristen could stay home and raise the baby. He hated the thought that someone else spent more time with his child then he and his wife did.

One thousand dollars, Michael's thoughts drifted back to one of the questions the speaker asked during his presentation. *What would I do with an extra thousand dollars a month?* For some people, maybe it didn't seem like much. For Michael, an extra thousand dollars a month, above and beyond what he was currently earning, would be life-changing. He started thinking about what he would do with the extra money.

He could pay that medical bill.

He could also get the tires he needed for his car.

Heck, he would sell the car and get one he could rely on.

How great it would be to start saving money again! Or just make an extra payment on his mortgage now and then and cut five or ten years of interest payments off his daunting thirty-year plan.

These things sounded ideal, but the one that trumped all others was that one thousand dollars a month just might be enough to bring his wife home from work, and enable her to stay home with their son. After factoring in all the money they spent on daycare, commuting expenses, clothing and supplies for her work, that amount was very close to what Kristen was taking home at the end of each month.

Yes, one thousand dollars a month would be incredible, but only if it came in the form of passive income. Michael knew he couldn't go out and get another job. He'd never see his family. Working more than he already was would just send him to an early grave. No, he couldn't earn that kind of money the conventional way. He needed to do it passively, like the speaker at the meeting talked about.

When their son was born, Michael and Kristen sat down with a financial planner to discuss options to better ensure they would be able to afford college, and hopefully, be able to retire at a reasonable age.

During that meeting, Michael learned that for them to earn a residual one thousand dollars a month, they would need more than $200,000.00 in the stock market. Of course, that's only in a good market earning at least five percent interest. That simply wasn't an option. He didn't have that amount of money to invest. If he did, the stock market had been so unreliable that he wouldn't want to take that chance.

There were other alternatives. A friend of Michael's had invested in a couple of rental properties. At first blush, he seemed to be doing well. The fact was though, he often complained about bad tenants, the stress of keeping up with repairs, ever increasing taxes and utility bills. When Michael would inquire about owning properties, his friend would often respond by saying something like, "It's not for everyone," or, "I spend more time and money working on those houses than I do my own."

Since Michael wasn't comfortable with a hammer in his hand, and he loathed the very idea of sinking hundreds of thousands of dollars in debt, owning properties didn't seem like a good solution for him either.

Not having the money, or quite honestly, the stomach to invest in the stock market or real estate often left Michael wondering how he was ever going to leverage himself. How could he find a way to earn more money without taking the kind of time away from his family that Kristen's father did? The most logical and reasonable solution seemed to be right in front of his face.

As he weaved through traffic, Michael continued to contemplate how earning just a little bit of money through a home-based business could give him his life back. If all that he ever accomplished was the elimination of the need for daycare, then that alone would be something worth celebrating. He already missed the first time his little guy said, *Dada*. He wondered if he would also miss the first time he crawled and walked. He fought to convince himself that the people at the daycare could be trusted. Sadly, it was mostly teenagers who worked there.

Would they really know what to do if there was a problem with Dylan? Nightmares of the recent hospital scare crept in his mind constantly, as it did Kristen's. He tried not to think of these things, but he couldn't help it. Any good father would react the same way. His current plan was not working. He was starting to understand that the true definition of "*insanity*" was doing the same things repeatedly and expecting different results.

Michael then thought of another question the speaker asked during his presentation. The question was simple: *are you earning what you're worth*? It was a sobering question that he answered as honestly as he possibly could—*I hope not!* He knew there must be a better way.

Making the Call

EVERY DAY AT WORK was difficult, both physically and mentally. This day was a particularly challenging one. Two employees had called out sick and Michael was expected to pick up their slack. He often felt it was unfair that he could significantly out-perform his coworkers and still bring home the same amount of money that they did. He was aware that if he factored in their seniority, his pay was actually less. His boss wasn't very good at recognizing the fact that Michael always put in more time, energy and effort than the others. This added to Michael's frustration.

To make matters worse, there seemed to be an inner circle of workers that had formed a high school-like clique. One he was clearly not a member of and most definitely did not want to associate with since their favorite activities were whining and complaining. The clique was convinced they had the answer to all of the country's problems and they never resisted the urge to voice their often absurd ideas. If Michael did not have to spend forty plus hours a week with them he might find them amusing. This certainly wasn't the case. He spent most of his waking hours with these people who gave merit to the phrase, "misery loves company."

Michael was grateful to have the job, but was less than thrilled that it happened to fit the definition of "dead-end job." There was little, to no, opportunity for promotion or increased pay. No recognition or appreciation for effort. No feeling of significance. He felt as expendable as a disposable razor. Nevertheless, he was dedicated, and that effort showed every day.

Although he had anticipated making the call, Michael's lunch hour was almost over before he finally mustered up enough courage to do so. It was strange that he never had a problem picking up his phone and calling people for social reasons, but the thought of making a call to Blake turned his cell phone into a living, breathing monster. He had been practicing what he was going to say in his mind all day. Although he feared he would fumble his way through the conversation, he took out his cell phone and dialed Blake's number. After the fourth ring, Michael was slightly relieved that Blake didn't answer. He was about to hang up when a powerful and commanding voice suddenly answered.

"Hello, this is Blake."

Michael's heartbeat instantly multiplied. "Hi... Um, Hello, Mr. Easton? This is Michael Harper. Tim Harper's son." There was silence. Michael continued, "We met a few years ago, at my father's funeral."

"Yes, Michael, I remember. How are you?"

"Well, I'm good, Sir. I was wondering if, well. When you handed me your card a few years ago, you said I could call if I needed anything and I, well. I..."

"Is everything okay?" Blake asked.

"Yes Sir, I just wanted to know if it was possible if I could get a few minutes of your time for advice on something."

"I'm busy today. Can you come by my office tomorrow?"

Michael didn't expect a response so quickly. He wasn't sure if he could get off work on such short notice, but he couldn't pass up this opportunity. "Sure, what time?"

"How does one o'clock work for you?"

"That would be great. Where should I meet you? I mean, where is your office?"

"It's at my house. Do you know where I live?" He answered.

"Actually, I believe I do. You live in Middletown, somewhere on the Navesink River, right?"

"That's right," Blake said, before giving Michael his actual address.

"So, I guess I'll see you tomorrow, Mr. Easton."

"Very good, see you then, and Michael, please call me Blake," the millionaire said, before hanging up quickly.

Michael wondered if he was wasting the busy millionaire's precious time. Did he have the right to ask this important man to spend a few minutes helping him? Regardless of his doubt, he was happy that he was going to have the opportunity to talk with a man who has achieved so much. Surely, he would benefit from their brief conversation tomorrow afternoon. Back to work he went, wondering what tomorrow would bring.

Michael didn't realize how sore his shoulders were from lifting and relocating hundreds of heavy boxes until he returned home. He could barely lift his arm long enough to unlock his front door. When he finally accomplished the task, he was happy to find Kristen on the couch feeding the baby. It was another sight he loved to see—a loving mother nurturing her son. Times like this were a reminder that he had the best wife on the planet. He also knew Kristen still considered him a wonderful husband and father, but he wanted to be a wonderful provider as well. Only then would he feel like he had lived up to the promises that he made to himself, Kristen, and even Kristen's mother, who he assured would never have to worry about her daughter's security and well-being.

He knelt down and gently kissed Kristen on the lips and with a soft hug and neck nuzzle, he greeted his baby boy "How was your day?"

"It was good sweetie," she answered with a smile. "How was yours?"

He wasted no time in sharing his news. "I called Blake Easton this afternoon."

"And?" Her eyes lit up. She wanted details.

"We're meeting tomorrow at one o'clock."

"Wow. That was quick. Aren't you working tomorrow?"

"My boss owes me some comp time. I'm working a half day and taking off at noon."

Michael immediately recognized the disappointing expression that took over his wife's face. It was similar to the one he had seen when she crumbled up the picture of that Coach bag and threw it in the garbage. He had an idea where this was going, but he knew he had to start the conversation, "What's wrong?" he reluctantly asked.

"I thought you were saving your comp time so we could extend our vacation this summer," she said as her eyes turned down toward the floor.

"Honey, you know my boss would never let me take comp time in August."

"What's the difference when you take the time? It's yours?"

Michael could feel his body tensing. "It's not my time," he said, trying to remain calm.

"Yes it is." she disagreed. "It's your time, and it's our time. I don't understand why you want to waste it tomorrow. Why can't you meet with Blake another time?"

Michael raised his voice to match his anxiety level "Because he offered to meet me tomorrow and I can't afford to pass up the opportunity!" he explained. "And it's not my time. It's my boss' time. I'm sick and tired of having to live my life on his time. He tells me when I have to work and when I can go home. He decides when, and if, I can take vacation and he determines how much I'm worth. I'm sick of it. I'm absolutely sick of it!" he bellowed.

Michael became so frustrated by speaking the truth, he pulled his work shirt over his head and threw it to the ground, leaving him in a sweat stained t-shirt. Dylan, obviously startled by the noise and tension, began to cry. Kristen comforted him as Michael took a few deep breaths and gathered his composure before continuing. They both knew that every heated discussion they have ever had revolved around work, money or lack of quality time together. The latter was usually a result of the former two.

"Honey, I have to beg, borrow, and steal for five hours of my time back. He even wanted to take vacation time away from me from when the baby was in the hospital because I didn't follow the company's family leave protocol—which I never knew existed in the first place." Michael explained as he knelt down in front of his wife and lovingly caressed the baby's head. She lifted her eyes to meet his, only to discover tears in them. "I can't keep doing this Kristen. I can feel myself dying. There has to be a better way. I'm at the end of my rope," he said.

Her eyes began to well up. She could see the pain in her husband. She raised her hand to wipe the tears off his face, wishing she could wipe away his troubles instead. Michael's expression said it all, but he still managed to get out the words, "I don't know what to expect when I sit down with this guy, but something is telling me that I have to do it."

"I know. It's alright," she said reluctantly. "Go. Meet with him tomorrow."

They hugged, with the baby safely between them.

"I love you," Michael said softly.

"I love you, too," his wife replied.

Neither of them reopened the discussion that evening. They had a nice dinner and a relaxing night in front of the television watching a sitcom. Michael wasn't laughing. Instead, his mind was on the following day. His hopes were that the meeting with Blake would somehow be a step in the direction he wanted his life to be headed. He also didn't want his expectations to be too high. He had been let down many times in the past and didn't feel he could handle much more disenchantment.

After Kristen went to bed, Michael pulled out a pamphlet he was handed that night at the hotel. It was titled, *Four Keys to Finding the Right Opportunity.* He thumbed through the pages and scanned the list, which read as follows:

1. The right corporate and field leadership.
2. The right product or service.
3. The right compensation plan.
4. The right timing.

Michael didn't know if this company had the right corporate and field leaders. That would be something he would only find out by attending more events like the one at the hotel and meeting people. However, he did know that they offered the right products and services. As far as the compensation plan goes, he was initially surprised by how much money the company was allowing people to earn. His job had a ceiling—this opportunity did not. The pamphlet stressed the fact that a person could earn as much as he or she wanted to as long as they put effort into it.

The fourth key to finding the right opportunity was timing. Michael was thirty and had less money in his bank account than he did ten years ago. He was living paycheck to paycheck and arguing with his wife over clipping coupons and turning the lights off when she left rooms. When it came to earning more money, timing could not be better. Still, if he was going to achieve financial relief with this opportunity, it would all come down to one person Michael. He simply didn't know if he had what it took to get the job done.

That evening, Michael laid in bed listening to the securing, steady rhythm of Kristen's peaceful breaths. His eyes were open, yet dreaming of the "what-if's." *What could I have done differently to prevent this mess? My family deserves so much better.* His mind raced. It was another sleepless night.

A Battle Within

THE SECOND HAND on that ugly round clock hanging over the door of his boss' office seemed to be moving in slow motion. Michael arrived early and was working hard, as expected. Today, he was watching time just like he did in high school when he was wrestling against the state champion. He kept one eye on the clock at all times. The difference this time, however, was that he wasn't on his back trying not to prevent getting pinned. The discouragement he encountered during that match was very much akin to that which he encountered on a typical work day.

At noon, Michael promptly punched out and entered the dingy locker room where he had placed his carrier bag earlier. He quickly changed out of his uniform into a pair of black dress pants and a light blue dress shirt. He wasn't surprised when he extended his arms and noticed the shirt sleeves were too short. He couldn't remember the last time he had worn it. *Perhaps at that wedding five or six years ago?*, he thought. Catching a glimpse of his poor image in the smudged locker room mirror didn't help him gain any confidence. The cheap mirror was aged and warped. Like one you'd see in a carnival funhouse. The flickering fluorescent light above his head completed his less than flattering portrait. He was embarrassed by his outdated clothing, but knew it was the best choice of apparel for meeting the millionaire.

Michael anticipated his co-workers' sarcastic remarks and cat calls as he exited the bathroom. He moved hastily and avoided eye contact. Moments after leaving the warehouse, he was in his car and on his way to meet the millionaire. Sweat was already forming on his brow.

Being hungry enough to feel your stomach growl is one thing. Hearing it growl is something different altogether. Michael did not want to be late, so he pulled into the McDonald's drive thru and waited behind two cars. He wasn't thinking so much about what he was going to eat. *A cheeseburger and fries would suffice.* Instead, he was more concerned with what the person at the pick-up window was going to think of him.

Last winter, Michael was driving down the Garden State Parkway. He pulled up to a tollbooth and rolled down his window to pay the toll. After dropping his coins in the bucket, he tried to roll his window up. It wouldn't budge! He drove the next twenty-two minutes, traveling sixty-five miles per hour, his window stuck in the down position. The temperature outside was thirty-one degrees, without the additional wind chill factor.

The next day, he covered the window with plastic and drove the car to the service center. There it was discovered that the power to the window shorted-out and needed rewiring. Of course, he didn't have the money to fix it, so he had the mechanic open the door panel, manually roll up the window, and reattach the panel as a temporary solution. Having the window stuck in the up position was the feasibly better option. Michael knew he wasn't going to have the window fixed anytime soon, if ever. As a band-aid to the situation, he went online and purchased an E-Z Pass. That took care of the toll problem, but did nothing to help him when he needed to roll down his window. This particular day was one of those times he needed help.

Normally, to avoid the embarrassment, Michael would just park the car and walk into a fast food restaurant to place his order. Being short on time, today that wasn't an option. Instead, he pulled up to the order station and opened his door to place his order. He followed the speaker's instruction and pulled around to the first window to pay for his food. On the opposite side of the window was a large man sitting on a stool wearing a headset. The man was waiting for Michael to pull up and pay while simultaneously taking another driver's order. Michael crept up to the window, then a little past it.

The man put his arm out to stop him from driving too far up, but Michael ignored the gesture. He pulled up just far enough—about two feet—so that he could open the door and reach back to hand the man his money. He was relieved that the man did not say anything. He didn't even crack a smile. He simply took the money and said, "Pick up at the next window." *One down, one to go,* Michael thought.

His celebration came to an immediate halt the moment he noticed there was a concrete curb directly under the second window. The curb was placed there for safety reasons. It prevented people from opening up their door, the very thing Michael needed to do. Another curb on the passenger side of the car kept him from being able to pull far enough away from the building so that he could open the door at all. This left only one alternative. His ritual usually embarrassed his wife enough for her to turn her head and cover her face. He was thankful that she wasn't with him this time and would be spared the humiliation. He pulled past the window again, this time about three feet. He gave a partial smile to the girl waiting to hand him his order as he slowly inched forward. He then rolled down the rear driver side window, lifted the recline lever on his seat and leaned back until he was in a full horizontal position. Once he was in position, he reached his arm toward the woman to grab his bag of food.

Being laughed at is one thing, but being laughed at by a teenage girl at a McDonald's drive-thru window is something different altogether. Without his dignity, Michael lifted his seat and quickly left the parking lot. He ate as he drove. Fast food wasn't his preference, especially since he wanted to begin to be more conscious of his nutritional choices. His main concern at the moment was reaching his destination on time. Today, he had a meeting with a multi-millionaire.

As Michael cruised down the parkway, a familiar feeling came over him. As far back as he could remember, there were times when he would get excited about the possibility that something great was about to happen. Unfortunately these times were short-lived. Before he could fully embrace that moment, he would become consumed with negative thoughts. His short-lived excitement would be replaced by fear, doubt and insecurity. What drove him to that familiar place? It was probably the incident at the drive thru, or maybe it was just the way his mind had become programmed. Michael began to think of all the reasons why he would never be able to succeed in a network marketing business.

First, he thought about how his three best friends had already said no. His wife was also reluctant. He knew these three people better than anyone else on earth. If they said no, who would say yes? Michael couldn't think of one single person. He then started to think about how nervous he became when talking to people about the idea of joining a network marketing business. He also began to wonder if he even had the time to do anything other than the things that already filled his plate. He was doing what he did best, rationalizing everything. What he didn't realize yet, was that this was the kind of thinking that kept him broke his entire life.

He was having a psychological battle within himself, which was nothing new. This time, however, he had somewhat of a breakthrough. Instead of unconsciously enabling these thoughts to invade his mind, he recognized what was happening and began to fight back.

"Why do I think this way?" he whispered.

It was as if he had been living his life on a roller coaster. Any time he would get excited about something, he found a way to talk himself out of the possibility that everything was going to turn out fine. He didn't have an answer to his own question, but it became apparent to him that more times than not, he was his own enemy. His negative self-talk was just one more terrible habit he would have to break.

Michael's mind continued to wander as he exited the parkway and drove alongside the Navesink River—an estuary that ran eight miles long through four of the wealthiest neighborhoods in New Jersey. Many famous people lived in homes on the Navesink. Perhaps the residents who received the most publicity were the 16 Atlantic bottlenose dolphins that made the river their home two years earlier, from June until the winter. Authorities believed the dolphins followed a school of baitfish from the ocean through Sandy Hook Bay.

As he passed the large homes, Michael reminisced about the footage he watched on news channels. His mind wandered, and he began to think about how spectacular it must have been to sit in your own back yard and watch the dolphins swim. He also thought about how cool it would be just to spend a day in the backyard of one of these gorgeous homes? *How impressive it is that someone from my old neighborhood is rich enough to live here?* It was apparent Blake Easton's daily mindset was vastly different from Michael's.

Drilling for Oil

EVERYONE FROM THE old neighborhood may have known where Blake Easton's home was, but very few of them had actually laid eyes on it. A large private fence surrounded the mansion. The front-side sat behind massive trees and shrubbery so thick, that no part of the home could be seen. If you owned a boat and traveled the river, you'd have an open view of the stunning yard, but the street-side was well concealed for privacy.

Michael arrived ten minutes early. He pulled into the driveway and stopped at the front gate, which was closed. Unsure what to do, he opened his door, placed one foot on the ground and looked for some kind of call button.

"Can I help you?" echoed a woman's voice from a small black speaker.

"Um, yes, I have an appointment with Mr. Easton." He answered.

"Mr. Harper?"

"Yes. That's me."

The gates parted in the center and began to open slowly inward.

"Make an immediate left and drive straight until you come to your first building. You can park in front and walk in," she directed, "I'll inform Mr. Easton that you have arrived."

"Thank you." Michael replied. He sat back in his seat, closed his door and looked up at a video camera that was directed toward him. Immediately, he wondered if the woman could tell that his window was broken. He let out a nervous chuckle prior to moving forward.

Before turning left as directed, he looked straight ahead, down a curved driveway and stretched his neck to get a peek at the millionaire's mansion. Shoot! It was hidden behind the trees. He could only imagine how magnificent it must be. He turned. Thirty yards down was a beautiful two-story building that was nicer than most homes he had ever been in.

"That's his office?" he whispered. "It's bigger than my house."

He parked his car in front of the building, next to a white Mercedes S class. He exited and took a moment to admire the vehicle. The shimmering sunlight reflected off the car in a brilliant way. Michael cautiously ran his hand on the hood and down the side of the car as he continued moving toward the front door. It felt as sleek as it looked.

He did as instructed and entered the building. A professionally dressed young woman sitting behind the front desk immediately greeted him.

"Good afternoon, Mr. Harper," she said, with a welcoming smile.

Michael recognized her voice as the one on the speaker at the front gate.

"Good afternoon to you." He replied, lifting his smile to match hers.

The woman extended her arm and pointed down the hall. "Mr. Easton is expecting you. He's the second door on the right."

Following her direction again, he began to walk down the hall. Hanging on the wall to the left was a series of posters with inspirational quotes on them. One of them featured a collage of famous athletes from the area. The caption underneath read, *big shots are little shots who kept shooting.*

"That's a great saying," he whispered, as he continued to walk down the hall.

On his right were large glass panels, forming a wall that revealed a fully-equipped gym. The gym consisted of a combination of cardio equipment and free weights. The far wall was a large floor-to-ceiling, wall-to-wall mirror. The mirror created the illusion of a larger room, but did not take away from the fact that this personal gym had everything you could ever want—an elliptical machine, treadmills, stationary bikes, a rowing machine, a full set of dumbbells, leg machines, a bench press and an upper body universal machine.

Continuing down the hall, he came upon another large glass window. Behind this one, was Blake's office. Through the window, he could see Blake Easton sitting at his desk, slowly shuffling through papers while talking on his telephone, pressed in between his shoulder and ear. The millionaire looked exactly like he did four years earlier, sporting his signature tan. Before Michael could knock on the door, Blake looked in his direction and waved him in. Michael entered, shut the door behind him and followed Blake's hand gestures to take a seat opposite him, with his back to the glass.

Covering the phone's mouthpiece, Blake whispered, "I'll be off in less than a minute."

"Take your time, Sir." Michael replied.

Michael took advantage of the opportunity to look around. He admired the office he was sitting in. It was definitely a place where he would expect an influential man to conduct business— a combination of class and power.

One wall was decorated with more than a dozen 16" X 20" matted photographs featuring various angles of beautiful sailboats. Some were close ups of the ship's bows with the shape of the boats fading in the background. Others highlighted classic sails and dramatic arches that were created by powerful winds. Each photo was a piece of art in terms of composition. The opposing wall featured photos of Blake and his wife on various vacations. One picture had the couple riding a gondola in Venice, Italy. Another showed them in front of the Roman Coliseum. There was a picture of them in front of Pyramids in Cairo, Egypt and a picture of the couple on the Sea of Galilee in Israel.

One photo showed them dressed in winter attire on the deck of an Alaskan cruise ship as they passed icebergs in the background. Several others had them in summer attire on the beaches of the world. Michael secretly marveled at the pictures of the couple posing in front of the Ritz Carlton in Spain, on the edge of the Grand Canyon, and at the Acropolis in Athens, Greece. The locations varied, but there was one thing that all of the photos had in common, the smile on their faces.

Opposite the glass and behind Blake was what appeared to be a constant stream of falling water. It took a moment for Michael to realize the waterfall was protected by a thick piece of glass. This is why he couldn't hear it. Hanging in the office, framed in gold, was a piece of paper with writing on it. On top of the paper in bold letters were the words "Mission Statement." Michael had heard of a mission statement before, but he wasn't exactly sure what one was. He squinted and tried to read the sentences below, but the letters were a little too small for him to see from where he was sitting.

On a three-foot high marble stand in the corner sat an impressive statue of a solid bronze eagle with wings extended upward and claws open. It was as if the eagle was swooping down to grab something. Michael could tell this was more than just a decoration. It was a trophy of some sort. On the base of the eagle were the words 'Top Producer.' It was dated twelve years prior to the current one, but the eagle looked brand new. This award was the obvious centerpiece of the office.

Blake found the paper he had been looking for and informed the person on the other end of the phone, "I have it in my hands right now. I'll have my assistant fax it to you after my meeting." Within seconds, he was off his call.

The millionaire looked up at Michael and studied him for a flash. Without looking away, he reached out and pressed the button on his phone that connected him to the woman at the front desk.

"Sheila, I'll be in a meeting. Would you please hold my calls?"

Realizing *he* was the meeting made Michael feel important, but awkward at the same time. He still wasn't sure if he was worthy of the millionaire's time.

"Hello Mr. Easton. Thank you for seeing me today," he said, launching the conversation.

"Please, call me Blake," the millionaire insisted. Without wasting a second, he continued, "So, tell me about yourself, are you married?"

"Yes, it'll be two years this December. Her name is Kristen. She's a fourth grade teacher."

"Terrific, do you have any children?"

"We do," Michael said, displaying a smile only a proud father could own. "My son, Dylan, turned eight months last Wednesday."

"Cherish the moments, they grow quick, believe me," Blake advised, "What line of work are you in?"

"I work as a machine operator in Jersey City. I've been with the company for seven years now." *Machine operator sounds a little better than laborer,* he thought.

"What made you choose that profession?"

After a brief silence, "I'm not exactly sure," he admitted, "I guess the profession chose me."

"Really, how so?" Blake asked, curiously.

"I needed a job," Michael explained. "It's tough to find a good one without a college degree—so when a friend told me they were hiring, well, I applied for the job and got it."

Michael was embarrassed. Not as much about his job, as he was about what he had just said. He realized that it sounded as if he settled for whatever came his way. Truth be told, he knew he did, but until this moment, he never openly admitted it. He was hoping to change the subject. Blake helped. "What do you do when you're not working?"

"Well, I like to spend as much time with my family as possible." Michael said, his smile returning. "We love the Jersey shore, so we take day trips to Point Pleasant Beach a couple times a month during the summer. Although with the baby, it's been difficult this past year."

"Do you ever travel outside New Jersey?"

"Not really, we'd love too... one day." *When we can afford it,* he thought.

Blake took a moment to absorb all the information that Michael had just provided. It was time to cut to the chase. "What prompted you to reach out to me?" he asked.

This is it... Michael took a deep breath. "I'm looking to make a change in my life." He admitted, feeling more comfortable than he had thought he would after sharing so much about himself with the millionaire. "I feel as if I'm at a stale mate and I came here to pick your brain and seek advice on a business, but if I'm wasting your time I... "

"What kind?" Blake interrupted.

Michael wrinkled his forehead. Confused, he asked, "Excuse me?"

"You said you were looking for a change. What kind of change?"

"Well," he pondered, "one that can help me achieve financial success, and I guess I wanted to talk with you because you're the most successful person I know. Well, sort of know."

"Success can be defined in many ways. I think I have a long way to go before I arrive, but thank you for the compliment."

Blake's response confused Michael, with a chuckle, he questioned, "A long way to go? If you're not successful, I can't imagine who is?"

Blake didn't flinch. Instead, he instantly came back with, "Michael, what is your definition of success?"

"Well, I'm not exactly sure, but a million dollars in my bank account would be a good start." He said in jest.

"I know plenty of people who have that, but have not achieved true success," Blake began, "Success is about more than just money. True success can only be attained when a person finds happiness and personal fulfillment. I believe this begins by defining the lifestyle you want to live, then taking the necessary steps and implementing a specific game plan to begin achieving that lifestyle. In other words, success is the progressive realization of a worthwhile goal or dream. You will not find success at the end of a journey by looking at a dollar figure. It's more than that. Success is something you become during a process."

Michael didn't fully understand what Blake was saying, but that was why he was there, to learn how successful people think. He tried to think of the right question to ask, but Blake beat him to the punch.

"What type of business are you looking at?" the millionaire asked.

Michael was reluctant to answer. He was concerned that Blake might have the same opinion that Dean and the others did about the network marketing industry, which would make him feel even more foolish for entertaining the thought about building the business. He also knew that he was occupying the time of an important man and he needed to respect that fact. So he did, "It's a network marketing company," Michael answered.

Blake didn't respond immediately, instead, a sly grin momentarily came over the millionaire's face, which concerned Michael. He wasn't sure what that grin meant, but it seemed clear that the millionaire looked down on network marketing. This gave Michael an uneasy feeling so he decided to shift gears. One of the main reasons why Michael wanted to meet with Blake in the first place was to hear the millionaire's story first hand, so he made the decision to change the subject. Perhaps he could still leave with some kind of inspiration.

"I was also wondering if you could tell me how you were able to accomplish so much."

Another smile, this one not so mysterious, informed Michael that Blake was happy to share. "I suppose it all started when I was five," he began, "We lived down the street from a small grocery store and I used to watch the women walk to the store and leave for home ten minutes later, carrying bags of groceries. One day I sat in front of the store with my wagon and as the women exited, I asked if I could carry their bags in exchange for a quarter. I was the envy of my street because I was the only kid on the block who always had money for gum, which I would buy and exchange for baseball cards and other items that I wanted."

"Wow, you were a regular Tom Sawyer," Michael said, matching Blake's smile.

"I learned early on, one key to achieving success is to find a need and fill it. It's one of the principles I've used to build my businesses."

"Some people who know you say you were destined to achieve great things." Michael said.

"Is that what they say?" Blake's face showed a hint of amusement. "I'm not sure about that. Perhaps I had gotten off to an early start, but by the time I reached high school, like every other teenage boy, I was more interested in girls than I was in money," he confessed. "I was just your average teenager... until May 9th."

The millionaire's demeanor instantly changed.

"May 9th?" Michael inquired.

"That's the day my father passed away. The day my whole world fell apart."

"I'm sorry... What did you do?"

"I dropped out of high school," Blake said, looking directly into Michael's eyes. "I'm not proud of that fact, but I had a sick mother at home and we needed money. There was no other option. At least, that's what I thought at the time. So I took advantage of any way I could find to make a buck. Paper routes. Painting. Cutting lawns. Shoveling snow. Whatever someone would pay me for, I'd do," Blake explained, before admitting, "I even did some things I'm ashamed of, but I was desperate."

Michael tilted his head. Confused, he asked, "Didn't you have any family that could help? I mean, financially?"

Blake chuckled, "My uncle told me I was an idiot for dropping out. He said I would never amount to anything." His smile faded, "After a while, if a person hears that enough, they start to believe it. When my mother passed later that year I was out of control, but that's about the time I met my wife and everything changed again, this time for the better."

Michael raised his eyebrows, "Really, how so?"

"She straightened me out," Blake said bluntly, "If it wasn't for her…" he smiled again, shaking his head and letting the thought just hang there. "I love that woman."

"So what happened?" Michael asked, with heightened curiosity.

"She encouraged me to believe in myself. Sometimes, all you need is one person to believe in you for you to change the direction of your life. But even when you find that person, nothing happens until you start to believe in yourself."

Michael leaned back in his chair and took a deep breath. He thought about his father who always encouraged him as a teenager, and then he thought about Kristen, and how supportive she was early on in their relationship. Perhaps his lack of belief in himself was the real reason why her attitude towards him, and life in general, had changed throughout the past few years. Could that be?

Michael wanted to absorb the millionaire's message. He sat back and pondered the thought and his eyes again connected with the majestic eagle award with Blake's name on it. Attempting to get his mind off his uncomfortable revelation, he asked the next question that came to his mind, "What made you want to be an entrepreneur?"

Without hesitation, Blake answered, "It goes back to the definition of success we just talked about. I wanted to be in business for myself. Even though I had found a job in sales and made a respectable living for more than five years, I was working all the time, and for someone else—my boss. I could have worked fewer hours, but then I'd be bringing home less money and struggling to make ends meet. I was looking for a way to earn as much, or more than I was making in sales without having to be away from home as much as I had been. My wife, Laura and I were newlyweds. We wanted to start a family. I knew there had to be a better way. It was around that time I met the second person who changed the direction of my life. He was a wealthy man I knew from my church and he taught me how to leverage my time and diversify my income."

Leverage and diversify were familiar terms for Michael. "I just learned about those two things myself a couple nights ago."

"Which company?" Blake asked.

"Excuse me?"

"The network marketing company you went to look at, which one was it?"

When Michael answered the question, Blake laughed. Again, Michael took this as a bad sign. He never expected to hear what came out of the millionaire's mouth next.

"Welcome to the team." Blake said, as he reached into his pocket, pulled out his money clip, removed a membership card and held it up.

Michael recognized the logo. It was the same as the one on the business card that the speaker at the meeting handed him. Of all the things Michael thought he might learn today, hearing that Blake Easton was involved in network marketing wasn't even a consideration. Perplexed, Michael questioned, "You're a member?"

"Yes."

"Did you just join?"

"Not exactly. Remember that man I talked about a moment ago, the one who taught me about diversification?" Michael nodded. Blake continued, "He brought me in more than twenty years ago."

Michael was shocked. "Well, I would imagine that with your credibility, you must have done pretty well." He commented.

"Back then," Blake scoffed, "What credibility did I have? I may have been doing okay, but everyone from high school knew me as the kid who dropped out. The only other people I knew were my customers. But you are right about one thing, I did well… very well as a matter of fact."

Michael couldn't help but to smile. He felt as if it was all beginning to make sense; the meeting at the funeral parlor, the timing of his recollection of that meeting, the preservation of Blake's business card. Maybe they were all signs. "Tell me more," he insisted, "What happened after you signed up?"

"I set my first goal. I wanted to make between one and two thousand dollars a month." Blake began. The number figure was very familiar to Michael, "I didn't do it my first month because I wasn't teachable."

"I don't understand," Michael admitted.

"What I mean is… I wasn't listening to what the successful people were trying to teach me to do. Although there was a proven system that all the top people were following, I thought I was smarter, so I tried it my way first. It was a humbling experience, to say the least." Blake admitted.

"What happened to make you change?"

"The man I told you about gave me a box of about forty cassette tapes and the book *How to Win Friends and Influence People*. He challenged me to listen to the tapes and read the book, and told me to come back to see him when I was finished. Thirty days later, I brought back the box and asked for another. He was shocked that I had done it so quickly."

"Forty cassettes in thirty days, that's more than one a day."

"This was the first time a self-made millionaire had ever given me advice for free. I would have been crazy not to do what he suggested. Wouldn't you agree?" Blake asked.

Michael raised his eyebrows and nodded his head. "Yes. That makes a lot of sense," he conceded. "What did the man say?"

"He didn't say much at all, but he gave me another forty and another book titled, *Think and Grow Rich*. Looking back, I realized this was a test to see how serious and self-motivated I was. The beautiful thing is that those cassettes and books changed the way I thought about almost everything. I immediately realized that for things to change, I had to change. At that point, I became teachable and listened to what people were telling me. I met with the top money earners in the business and asked questions. Then I did what they told me to do. That's when I started to become a student of success. By my third month, I was making more money part time than I was in my full time job."

"I'm sorry, but this is incredible," Michael interrupted. "How far did you go in the business?"

"I made millions," Blake said bluntly. Michael's mouth dropped. "I've had a long illustrious career with this company. Sure, I faced all kinds of adversity, but I aggressively built my team for two years before I reached the top level."

Michael was still trying to process everything he had just heard. "I don't understand?" he admitted, "The lifestyle you live today is a direct result of network marketing?"

"That's right. Of course, as time went on I diversified, but it all started with a simple, home-based business. The same exact one you have just been presented with."

Michael couldn't conceal the shocked look on his face. "Are you still involved?" he asked.

"I absolutely am still involved, but not the way I was back then. I still earn more weekly than I used to make monthly in my previous job. Those residuals are a direct result of the time I spent in the field. Over the years, however, my role has changed. Today I spend less time in the living rooms and more time in the boardrooms. I've served on a bunch of committees, coached others who are industry leaders today and traveled throughout the country for years as a consultant. In the process, I've met a lot of dynamic people and opportunities began presenting themselves, including investments in real estate and the opportunity to buy and sell stocks and businesses, which had been a dream of mine for many years. I just used the success principles that I learned in network marketing and applied them in my other business ventures. Those principles helped me succeed in everything else I have ever done with my life."

Michael's thoughts drifted to images of what the man in front of him must have looked like when he dropped out of high school. Certainly, it was not a mirror reflection of what Blake Easton was today. He couldn't help but to think about their old neighborhood, which was dead center in one of the most densely populated counties in America, houses on top of houses, a dollar store on every corner. A blue-collar community that was famous for, well, not much at all. Then he thought about where Blake Easton lived now. His neighbors were wealthy—very wealthy, and many of them were known throughout the entertainment and business communities.

"From where you came from to where you are today, you've achieved so much. You're truly living the American dream," he observed.

"Denis Waitley said, 'Success in life comes not from holding a good hand, but in playing a poor hand well.' I happen to agree." Blake explained, "And about that college diploma you mentioned earlier. The one you feel is so important. The way I look at it, a diploma is like a sticker on a suitcase, it shows where you've been, not where you're going."

Michael took another moment to contemplate what he had just heard. Everything that Blake was saying made sense. The millionaire summed up his feelings with the following, "Michael, if you want to try something new, you certainly don't need my approval, but let me share one of my favorite phrases. If you have nothing to lose by trying, and everything to gain if successful, by all means, try. If you succeed, you will end up developing a passive-residual income, which is similar to a life insurance policy. The difference, of course, is residual income pays you dividends while you are still alive."

Even though Michael didn't say anything, Blake's last comment made him think about his father. What he didn't realize was that, after a moment of reflection, it had the same effect on the millionaire. This became evident with Blake's next words.

"Michael, I have found it to be very rewarding any time I can help another person achieve their dreams and goals. For the past few years, I have only worked with the top people in this industry. However, out of respect for your father, I'd be honored to help you. I will not build your business, but I will disclose industry secrets that only those who have achieved tremendous success have come to understand. I think you would be making a very wise choice to take advantage of network marketing, and if you are willing to work, I can teach you what it takes to succeed in this industry."

"You would do that for me?" Michael asked, "Why?"

"During the great depression, there was an elderly gentleman who owned a big piece of property in Texas. He was in the process of filing for bankruptcy." Blake began. Michael wasn't sure if the millionaire heard his question. He continued to listen. "This man had lived on this land his entire life. It had been inherited and passed down to him through several generations. One day, some businessmen approached him and said they would like to drill on his property because they thought there might be oil underneath. Initially he said no, because he thought this might decrease the value of his property, but after speaking to his wife, the couple decided they had nothing to lose. They figured they were going to lose this piece of property anyway so they agreed to let the oil company come in and start the process.

Within days, they struck what turned out to be the largest oil well in our country's history. Instantaneously, this elderly man went from being poor to becoming a multimillionaire."

"Wow," Michael replied. "Talk about lucky."

"Was he lucky?" Blake asked, "If he owned this land his entire life, was he now just becoming a millionaire, or had been a millionaire his entire life, and just not known that all he had to do was to tap into what was already there?"

Michael didn't answer immediately. Instead, he once again began thinking about how many times in the past he had easily had dismissed the possibility that he could succeed at doing things that seemed out of reach. Before he could say a word, Blake continued. "I recognize that you have what it takes to succeed and perform at a much higher level than you ever thought possible, you just don't know it yet. So what do you say? Are you ready to tap into it?"

The look in Michael's watery eyes answered the question for him. The man he was sitting across the table from had just offered to become his mentor. It wouldn't be until much later that Michael would find out that there was a much deeper reason why Blake was taking him under his wing.

9

Paycheck to Paycheck

EVERY PERSON EXPERIENCES moments when they are burdened with anxiety or self-doubt. Some spend their entire lives feeling inadequate to such a degree that it handicaps them. Michael had become one of those people. Although he was encouraged by what had just transpired with Blake, his face carried the expression of uncertainty.

The millionaire was an expert at reading peoples' expressions and body language. He also understood that as quickly as a person turns a page in a book, is as quickly as their emotions can shift.

"You seem to have reservations?" Blake observed.

Michael briefly tilted his head back and closed his eyes. He was searching for the correct words, but allowed himself to say the first ones that came to mind, "I just don't know if I'd be good at it."

Blake glanced at the impressive eagle statue. Then subtly lifted his finger and pointed. Even though his hand movement was slight, the lighting in the room reflected off his watch and diamond ring, causing them to sparkle.

"Do you see that?" the millionaire asked.

Michael looked at the statue, "Yes, it's beautiful. I noticed it when I walked into your office."

"Do you know why I received that award?"

"Yes, it says 'top producer.' You must have made the most sales." Michael answered.

"That's partially true. I was *good* at selling, but not great. However, I learned a long time ago, that if I surround myself with people who are as good as, or better than I am at doing the things I am trying to accomplish, I dramatically increase my chances of achieving my goals. I earned that award because I led a team that made more sales than any other team in our company."

The millionaire waited for Michael to turn squarely in his seat and face him again before continuing, "The reason why you are struggling financially is because you are one man working one job for one salary. Employees don't create wealth or financial security for themselves, only for their boss. J. Paul Getty once said, 'I would rather have one percent of one-hundred people's efforts than one-hundred percent of my own.' He was one-hundred percent correct."

"Do you think working a job is foolish?" Michael questioned.

"You know," Blake began, "For many years I thought the key to success was to get a good job, work hard, seek promotion, save as much as I can, and retire after forty years with a nice gold watch and a social security check. Well, I learned very early on that J-O-B is an acronym for *just-over-broke*. Most people are surviving paycheck to paycheck, hoping for the best. To answer your question, I wouldn't say that working a job is foolish. People need to earn money so they can live. Relying solely on a job, yes, that's foolish. My best advice for a person in your situation is to continue to work full-time on your job, while investing part-time into your fortune."

"I like what you're saying, but I work five, sometimes six days a week. When I come home, I'm exhausted. As it is, I only have nine or ten hours a week that I could spare," Michael admitted.

"How does that make you feel?" the millionaire asked firmly. Michael was not prepared for this question.

"Excuse me?"

"You're telling me that you don't have any time, yet you're working all those hours, and still struggling to make ends meet." Blake summarized, "How does that make you feel?"

"Well... terrible, I guess."

"Good. It should make you feel terrible." Blake said bluntly.

Michael wasn't certain whether to be insulted or not.

Blake continued, "Now that you recognize the fact that your circumstances make you feel terrible, the only thing left to do is change those circumstances. You can do that by investing your time in ways where you can get that time back in abundance and earn substantial income in the process. You may only have ten hours a week to dedicate to your business, but when you duplicate yourself through the efforts of ten others who are also putting ten hours a week into their business, you will have one hundred and ten hours a week going into your business, even though you will still only be putting ten in yourself. Make it your goal to build an army of ambitious, like-minded people. By doing so, you will begin to duplicate your efforts and increase your chances of achieving the life you desire."

"*Ahh*, I get it," Michael said. "But I'm a little confused. Earlier, you said you invested in real estate and businesses."

"That's correct. I diversify."

Michael nodded as if to say he understood, but a curious look remained on his face. He was thinking, but not talking. Blake knew there was a question he was reluctant to ask.

"Go on," the millionaire prodded.

"I was just wondering. How do you balance everything?"

Blake smiled, "First, I love what I do. When a person does something they love for a living, they will never work a day in their life. I never pursued money. I pursued success in a career that I love. I only invest in businesses that have a proven system and allow me to leverage my time."

"What is a proven system?"

"Well, take network marketing for example. It's a proven business model that presents answers to two of the biggest reasons why traditional businesses fail." Blake lifted his hand motioning his fingers simultaneously to signify the two reasons… "A lack of money and a lack of business knowledge." Blake placed both his hands on his desk and leaned forward. "The startup costs are minimal compared to traditional business. If you wanted to start a traditional business, you'd most likely want to start a franchise because they also have proven systems. When you walk into McDonald's, where are the fries?"

"To the left," Michael answered.

"That's right, and they know exactly when to pull those fries out too. They have consistently followed the same system. It doesn't matter if you are in China or America, the fries taste the same." Blake leaned back in his chair. "That's an example of a proven system, but if you wanted to own a franchise, you would need hundreds of thousands of dollars. In some cases, millions, to get in on one. In network marketing, you spend less to join than you would for a new television.

Comparably, I am yet to come across any traditional business model that would require less than a hundred thousand to start. When it comes to knowledge, many people outside of our industry don't know where to turn when they're faced with business-related challenges. Their competitors aren't going to come to their aid. On the other hand, in network marketing, you have a team of people who will help you because they have a vested interest in your success. Additionally, you have access to answers of any questions you could think of, and solutions to whatever challenges you may encounter. There is information out there—teaching you what you need to do, in order to overcome the obstacles. That's what a proven system is, or what I like to refer to as the *"great equalizer"*. No matter who you are or where you come from, you can follow in the footsteps of those who came before you and succeed. They will teach you how to start your business, how to contact other people, how to follow through and how to reach whatever level you desire. The system alone should essentially remove any concerns you may have, but if it doesn't—think of all the other advantages that network marketing offers."

"Such as?" Michael was intrigued.

Blake summarized, "The ability to earn a full-time income on a part-time basis. The advantage of working with your spouse toward a common goal. The opportunity to develop an income that you can transfer to your children. It's the easiest way I know where a person could duplicate their efforts, without having to provide employee benefits, or pay franchise fees. Simply stated — a smart way to make a transition from being an employee to being a financially independent business owner."

Michael didn't allow himself to forget that he had a limited amount of time to learn from Blake. He glanced at his watch. In his mind, he chuckled when he remembered that under the scratched glass surface was a face that had been stuck on the time 3:20 for more than a month. Even though he was aware that his watch was busted when he put it on, it was the only one he owned, He just wanted to look more professional for his meeting with the millionaire. Apart from feeling foolish, he still felt that this would be a great time to ask for advice on how to overcome what appeared to be the most common objection and misconception about the industry.

"Some people say network marketing is a pyramid. Is that true?"

Without hesitation, the millionaire answered, "It's important to understand that those people aren't referring to illegal Ponzi schemes when they make that assumption. If so, they are talking from a place of ignorance.

"There are many skeptical and cynical people in this world, but there's a difference between the two. Skeptical people gather facts before they make an intelligent decision. I believe such skeptical people make great businessmen and women. Cynical people, on the other hand, make decisions without any facts.

"It's been my experience that cynical people are usually broke. Don't waste your time trying to educate or motivate the self-proclaimed know-it-all. Cynical people basically aren't interested in doing what it takes to succeed. They prefer to spend their time and effort trying to find ways to prevent others, like you, from succeeding. Whatever creative energy they have left is spent justifying why they are not willing to get off the couch and out of their own comfort zone.

"The easy way for them to do it in this case, is to throw out the word "pyramid", because it's easy and convenient. When you think about it though, Corporate America is the real pyramid in our society. Take any traditional brick and mortar business for example. Employees never earn more than the owner of the company will, unless they diversify. It goes back to that one percent of one hundred people's efforts illustration we talked about earlier."

Blake continued, "In most professions, a person earns a specific dollar amount regardless of individual effort. Network marketing has no limit. A person can earn what they want, and it doesn't matter when they were introduced to the company, where they are positioned or who they are. What makes network marketing more unique than any other business or sales model is that you have that opportunity to duplicate yourself. In a sense, it's like personal franchising."

Michael was encouraged. In a relieved manner he proclaimed, "That's good." He paused and said, "Now all I have to do is figure out where to begin."

"That's easy," Blake assured. "Let me start by asking you two simple questions. First, do you want to build your business fast or slow?"

"Fast," Michael answered.

"And do you want to build your business big or small?"

"Big."

"Great," Blake commended, "Now, during this process, you focus on building teams of people. To build a team, you have to take your eyes off yourself and focus on others. People will not follow you if they think you are more interested in achieving your dreams than you are in helping them achieve theirs. Have you ever read *How to Win Friends and Influence People* or *Think and Grow Rich?*"

"No," Michael replied.

"You are going to want to pick up a copy of both and read them as soon as possible."

Michael cringed. "I'm not a good reader," he admitted.

"That will have to change." Blake said bluntly. "Start with fifteen minutes a day, then increase to twenty. Soon you will be reading a book a month, then two. And I guarantee you will become better in all areas of life."

Michaels showed a hint of skepticism. He tried to conceal his expression before Blake noticed, but it was too late.

"Michael, in order to learn the things you don't know, you have to actively seek answers. Positive, self-help books provide the types of answers you are looking for. Think of it this way. The problems you are having in your life will never be solved by the same thinking that put you there in the first place. Don't you agree?"

Michael nodded, "Yes, I do."

"Great... here's what you need to do to start building your team. The first thing you want to do is make a list of two hundred and fifty people who you know and like, then..."

"Two hundred and fifty?" Michael interrupted on impulse. It was a knee-jerk reaction that he regretfully couldn't stop.

Blake was amused by the response. This was evident by the slight chuckle that came from his mouth, perhaps a knee-jerk reaction of his own. He had been working with industry leaders for so long that he had momentarily forgot about the learning curve that is present in someone who is starting in network marketing with little to no confidence. After achieving such a high level of success, it was easy for the millionaire to sometimes dismiss the mental anguish that some people who are making a names list go through when they mistakenly think they don't know anybody.

"Michael, if I told you I was going to give you one hundred dollars for each name you put on a list, do you think you could come up with 250 people who you know?"

This question caused Michael to think harder about whether or not he knew 250 people. "Yes," he answered, but he was still unsure if he knew that many.

Blake continued, "The fact is, you already know enough people to achieve the top level of this organization, and even if you didn't, you would meet enough people along the way to do so. Don't over think. I didn't ask if you knew 250 people you thought would want to do this, I only said 250 people that you know. I bet you have more than sixty programmed into your cell phone right now."

The millionaire was right. Michael had seventy-three numbers programmed into his cell phone. Blake then offered more valuable advice, "If you find yourself struggling to come up with names, use a list building tool like the 'Memory Jogger' that will come in your starter package. Scan through the professions that are listed in alphabetical order. Ask yourself who you know that is in the accounting business, or works for the airline industry. By the time you get half way through that list, you'll easily reach 250."

Michael took a mental note of what Blake had just said before asking, "What do I do after I make my list?"

"That's when you start to build your team. Begin by contacting your immediate up-line."

With a puzzled look, "What's an up-line?" Michael asked.

"This is the person who is going to sign you up, and come to your home to help you with your first couple of meetings. He will thoroughly explain the system we just spoke about, which you are going to follow when you begin to invite people you would like to be in business with, like your friends, to come look at the program."

My friends, Michael thought. Reality set in. His three best friends already made it clear they were not interested. He began to wonder out loud, "Billy already said no, and so did Dean. I doubt I'd be able to convince them…"

Cutting him off Blake clarified, "Don't convince. Amateurs convince, professionals sort. Do you think Bill Gates had to convince people to come and work for him and have an opportunity to become part of one of the most successful companies in the world?"

"No."

"Then you shouldn't either. Don't ever forget that you are offering something more than Bill Gates did for the majority of his employees, a chance at becoming financially free. The financial rewards a person can achieve in our industry are ones that everyone needs, but you're looking for people who want it, not people who need it. There's a difference," the millionaire explained. "You mentioned your friend Billy. Why did he say no?"

Other than the fact that Billy is obsessed with sports, Michael knew his friend hated the thought of being left behind. Even if Billy were in the loop, if he wasn't the center of attention, he would do what he could to sabotage the person who was. "I think he only likes to do things that are popular." Michael replied. "When everyone else is doing it, he'll want to do it too."

"A follower," Blake summarized, "Nobody ever became successful doing what the crowd does. The crowd is average. That's why they're called the crowd. If you want to be successful, you have to have a showdown with the calling of the crowd. Being a pioneer pays better than being a follower, trust me. Remember, you want to sort. Even if Billy was interested, it sounds like he may not be the one you're looking for. Move on to the next one, then the next one after that and continue the process until your team begins to form. A few months after I signed up, I showed the business to Mark. He was one of my best friends. I thought he would be great at it. However, instead of signing up, he told me the business looked good but he was convinced it wouldn't last five years. He told me I was wasting my time."

"What did you say?"

"I didn't say anything. I was still new and not very seasoned when it came to overcoming objections. Part of me thought he might be right. But one of the first things I learned was how to sort through prospects, so I put him in the 'not now' category. I actually ran into him about ten years later. He asked if I ever made any money with the business. I told him I had made millions. He was blown away."

"After he kicked himself, I'm sure he signed up and ran hard with it." Michael said.

"Actually, he didn't," Blake revealed. "He was convinced that it was too late to get in because most of the people he knew were already on my team. He was great at making excuses, but he actually taught me a valuable lesson."

"Which is?"

Blake answered, "The best revenge is massive success. If I had listened to him, I'd still be working paycheck to paycheck today. Instead, I followed a proven system to the 'tee' and the results speak for themselves. Michael, I'll say it again. Don't over think it, just make that list, invite people to look at the business and let them choose themselves."

"Understood," Michael replied. He was grateful to have received such wise counsel. Michael felt he had occupied enough of the millionaire's precious time. Blake had graciously provided him with indispensable advice. He was ready to get started. "I can't thank you enough for taking the time to meet with me today. It means a lot."

"It was my pleasure. I hope you found my words helpful."

"Definitely," Michael assured.

He placed his hands on his knees and leaned forward in his chair, getting ready to rise. Blake picked up his phone and pushed the button on the key pad that connected him to his assistant.

"Sheila, can you prepare a box of twenty-five audios for Michael."

Michael smiled. The millionaire put the phone down. Michael stood and reached across the desk to shake his hand. Blake rose to meet him. As their hands connected, Michael flashed his eyes toward the photos on the wall and commented on the ones of Blake and Laura, "You and your wife have traveled to places that most of us only read about."

It was a sincere remark.

Blake glanced at the photos, then back at Michael. His eyes widened momentarily, the way a young boy's would after his parents asked if he would like to go for ice cream. Blake quickly regained his composure as he released his grip and held up his index finger, an obvious gesture meant to suspend Michael. The millionaire opened a drawer to his desk and shuffled through papers until he found and pulled out a three-page brochure. He held it up for Michael to review. On the cover was a picture of a gorgeous yacht.

"Wow. Now that's a boat," Michael said.

Blake smiled. Only someone who wasn't familiar with yachts would refer to one as a boat. He did not intend to embarrass the young man, "This is the company brochure. They built my new yacht. That's it on the cover. It was delivered three weeks ago."

This didn't surprise Michael. "I'm sure it's gorgeous," he remarked.

Blake handed the brochure to Michael. "You can have it if you like… the brochure, not the yacht," he joked.

Michael opened it and glanced at the photos inside. Blake came around the desk and placed a hand on his shoulder, "If you're not doing anything on Sunday and you're in the area of Sea Bright, come by and see her. I'll be taking a few of our company's top leaders out for a couple hours on a test run. It would benefit you to spend some time around these people."

Michael wasn't sure what to say. *Am I dreaming or did Blake Easton just invite me on his yacht?* "You don't have to ask me twice," he replied.

"Then I'll see you at noon," Blake confirmed, "She's docked at the marina next door to McLoone's Restaurant." The millionaire narrowed his eyes and pointed at Michael. "Besides being on time, there are a few things you must do in order to get on this yacht."

"Anything," Michael said.

"I want you to listen to ten CD's, make that list of 250 people, and have your first home meeting. Regardless of the results, these are the things you have to do before you step foot on my yacht. Agreed?"

Michael breathed a sigh of relief. "Agreed," he answered.

Curiously, Blake asked, "What did you think I was going to ask you to do?"

"It's not that," Michael replied, "I thought you were giving me cassette tapes, not CD's. I wouldn't know what to play them on. I've never even seen a cassette player."

Blake laughed, "Believe it or not, I've kept up with technology since the day I was given those 40 cassette tapes."

The millionaire walked Michael to the office door before they parted ways. At the reception area, Michael accepted the box of CD's from Sheila.

Michael sat down in his car and sat for a moment, daydreaming of sailing on Blake's yacht. Before he could put the keys in his ignition, goose bumps invaded his body. He was actually invited on a multi-millionaire's yacht. His friends would never believe it, nor would his wife. He drove off, but stopped at the front gate. He reached his hand into the box, randomly pulled out a CD entitled, "Building Your Network Marketing Business," by Jim Rohn and inserted it. Before leaving the property, he turned his head and glanced down the driveway and again tried, unsuccessfully to see what Blake's house looked like.

10

Embrace the Struggle

MICHAEL'S FIRST MEETING with the millionaire influenced him greatly. He shared all the details with Kristen, and then called the person who invited him to the original business presentation. It was time to sign up. His emotions were all over the place. He was excited...then doubtful...then excited again...then unsure. That was only the first twenty minutes. He made the decision to move ahead, regardless of the emotional rollercoaster he was on.

While driving to and from work, he continued to listen to the CD's Blake gave him, thoroughly enjoying the refreshing, positive outlook that the speakers shared. Just as Blake instructed, he also began making his list using the *Memory Jogger*. Kristen hoped this was going to provide some type of financial reward, but the past experiences she had with her parents left her jaded. She was reluctantly supportive.

With the help of his up-line, Michael completed his application, scheduled his first meeting, and invited people over to his house to view the business opportunity. To prepare, he listened to the "Getting Started CD" and read the accompanying material that came in his starter package. The material highlighted the three things a person would have to master in order to build a profitable business, which were "The Invitation." "The Presentation," and "The Close." Michael especially focused on the part he needed the most help with—The Invitation. This also happened to be the most important of the three, because without a proper invitation, it's nearly impossible to get a prospect to the presentation, let alone close him.

The starter package came with sample scripts to guide him through a conversation. The key, of course, was not to engage in too much conversation. His goal was to create enough curiosity, and excitement, hoping someone would commit to viewing the presentation.

Michael scanned down his list and chose who he felt were his six key people. They were six friends he had known since grammar school. They were guys that he called upon many times for a variety of reasons. He was confident that they would agree to come over and see what he was excited about.

As he dialed the first number, he suddenly became uncomfortable. He was used to calling these guys and asking if they wanted to get together and play baseball or help a buddy move, not look at a way to get financially free. He tried, unsuccessfully, to ignore the anxiety that had unexpectedly come over him. It was an odd feeling, but Michael knew that he had to do this, so he began dialing numbers with the intention of inviting his friends over to his house for the 8:00 presentation the following evening.

The first three people he called immediately began asking questions. Michael felt obligated to answer them, so he responded emotionally with his own answers, not using words suggested by his up-line or the training material. They immediately rejected the invitation, making excuses, "This just isn't a good time for me, I have a lot on my plate right now." And "I have friends who tried something like this and it didn't work." Michael remembered Blake's comments about cynical people making decisions before they get facts. It made him think long and hard about the types of people he had been hanging out with most of his life. Were they really that negative?

The other three people he called said they would try to show up, which put his mind at ease. He would be happy settling for three at this point.

The next morning, Michael drove to work thinking about how great it would be to sign up three people. Although he did not have much confidence in himself, he did have confidence in Blake Easton, the business, and his up-line. He expected it to be a great night. However, before noon two of the three sent him text messages saying they were not going to be able to make it. One of them stated *something came up*.

Maybe it was the fact that he was having another difficult day at work, or perhaps it was the way the cancellation came in the form of a text. Whatever the reason, the message irked him. *What does that mean?* He questioned. *Something came up?* It seemed like such a deliberate blow-off. If the person said he had a family emergency or had to stay late at work, Michael would have understood, but he knew when he was being shunned.

Throughout the rest of his shift, Michael drove the forklift and contemplated the situation. Maybe becoming wealthy was unrealistic. After all, a manual laborer is where he is for a reason. He considered calling his up-line and cancelling the meeting, but there was still one person confirmed for the night. Maybe he should call that person also and let him know the meeting was going to be rescheduled, but if he did that, in his heart, he knew he probably wouldn't ever reschedule.

While clocking out, Michael mentally prepared for an uncomfortable drive home. His mind was full of questions. How was he going to tell his wife what happened? Should he call Blake and tell him he was thinking about cancelling? If he did, would the millionaire still mentor him? Would he still be invited onto the yacht? How would he feel on the yacht with all these millionaires when he couldn't even get people to look at the business? Would he feel inadequate being in their presence?

Why is everything I try to do so hard? he snarled under his breath.

He was about to pull out of the parking lot when he looked down at the box of CD's that Blake gave him. Part of him wanted to throw the box out of the window and forget about the entire thing. Another part of him felt that he needed to listen to another one. He reached in and pulled out a handful. Shuffling through them, he found one that looked interesting.

Might as well, he said, as he reluctantly placed the CD into his player. For the first few minutes, Michael wasn't even listening. His mind was too pre-occupied with the negative thinking that had consumed him over the past few years. Then something was said that captured his attention. "Every truly great success story can be divided into three parts: the dream, the struggle and the prize. It all begins with a *Dream*, followed by a *Struggle*, and the *Prize*. Those who overcome their struggles move on to claim their *Prize*, those who can't remain average. Most people quit during the struggle, and the struggle can be anything, a lack of time, lack of confidence, inability to overcome criticism, anything. A wise person will expect struggles every time he or she steps out of their comfort zone. They will not only expect it, they will embrace it because they know the prize they are looking for will be found on the other side."

The words came at the right time. Michael turned up the volume. "Strength does not come from winning. Strength comes from enduring and overcoming challenges. There is suffering in life, and there are defeats. No one who has ever achieved greatness has done so without them. You will never know what you were capable of becoming if you didn't face and overcome some form of adversity while on your journey."

Maybe struggles are part of the process, Michael thought.

He felt as if he was out of his league, but everything he listened to reassured him that this was normal. He didn't know what to do next, but one thing was for sure, he was NOT going to cancel his first home meeting. He would never be able to look his wife in the eyes if he did, nor Blake for that matter.

It was 8:15 when the doorbell rang. Michael breathed a sigh of relief. His only prospect showed up. Even though his friend sat there with his arms and legs crossed, said very little, and left without showing any interest whatsoever, Michael was not completely disheartened. He was disappointed, but he didn't have a no-show.

That evening, he and Kristen spoke about the cancellations.

"I must have done something wrong," he conceded.

"No you didn't," Kristen replied, "I just think it's harder to build this type of business in our area than it is in other places."

Michael shrugged, "Maybe you're right."

Even though the meeting did not produce the results Michael was hoping for, he was still looking forward to his first voyage on a yacht and his second meeting with the millionaire.

Now You Know

IT WAS EARLY Sunday afternoon. Most people had already reached their destinations for the day. Traffic was low, which made the drive down to the Jersey Shore a pleasant one. Michael had previously accepted an invitation to play golf with Billy, Dean and Tom, but he cancelled last minute. There was a brief instant where he questioned his decision, but then he negated his uncertainty by remembering a quote from one of the CD's, *I will do today what others will not, so I can do tomorrow what others cannot.* Spending a day on a yacht was hardly a difficult decision. Rubbing elbows with a handful of millionaires, however, was unfamiliar, and a slightly uncomfortable step for the blue-collar laborer.

When he reached the shore, Michael exited the turnpike and avoided local highways. He drove toward the ocean, down the coast passing through beachfront communities that he never knew existed. The homes were spectacular in size and design, each endowed with awe-inspiring views of the ocean. He couldn't help but wonder how these people could afford such expensive multi-million dollar estates, especially considering that most of them were vacation homes.

Truth be told, he felt a bit inadequate, yet at the same time, he was grateful that he had been given the opportunity to spend the afternoon with one of the wealthiest men in the state. Michael didn't know this before meeting with Blake, but two days ago, he did an internet search, and discovered that Blake and his wife were renowned throughout the yachting world, predominately because they owned not one, but two yachts. One of which was a 185-foot beauty called *The Visionary* was currently listed among America's 100 largest yachts. The one he was going to see, however, was not *The Visionary*. This was the newest member of Blake's growing fleet, named *The Majestic Treasure*.

Michael arrived at the Marina. He parked his car in front of McLoone's' Restaurant, opened his door, and instantaneously drew a deep breath. The air was different. It was refreshing and sterile, and with the right breeze, carried a wonderful scent of brine. He stepped out, stretched his body and began to walk toward the main dock, which was well-hidden behind the restaurant.

Michael loved the shore, just being near the ocean made him feel different—more alive. When he was a teenager, he thought that being a full-time lifeguard would have ranked high on his list of greatest jobs on earth. There was something about the ocean's energy. It represented life, tranquility and security.

Before he met Kristen, Michael used to keep a beach chair in the trunk of his car, and hoped to stumble upon time that he could dedicate to his earlier goal of becoming a beach bum. One evening, six years ago, he found time to do just that. Michael was driving through Belmar towards Point Pleasant beach to celebrate his friend Ryan's birthday at a club called *Jenks* when, for some reason, he suddenly came to the realization that the club scene had completely lost its appeal.

Out of character, he pulled off the road, took his beach chair out of his trunk, and carried it down to where the sand and water intertwined. He opened the chair to a slight recline and sat alone on the secluded beach. It didn't take long before he began to relax. He took off his shoes and placed his feet in the sand, curling his toes to feel its soothing texture. The waves methodically crashed on the beach, almost in slow motion—splashing a cool mist across his body and face. The moonlight reflected off the ocean in a soft, even glow.

Lost in his own world, a tiny bird captured his attention. He watched the bird run in and out, avoiding the waves from the evening tide. Michael closed his eyes and the entire world faded away. The only energy left was the sound of the waves and feeling of the mist on his face. It felt as if he was being kissed by God. The moment, however, ended when an elderly couple, who were enjoying a leisurely walk on the beach passed by and unintentionally woke him from his drowse.

Michael spent the better part of an hour on the beach that night, but he still wanted to do the right thing, so he decided it best to meet his friends at Jenks to celebrate Ryan's Birthday.

As fate would have it—that night—Michael met Kristen. She was on summer break from her teaching job, working as a waitress to help pay rent. To this day Michael tells his wife that if he didn't stop at the ocean and reawaken himself, he probably would never have assembled enough courage to ask for her number. She still affirms that it was the first time she had ever given her number out to a customer and only did so because of an unexplainable divine intervention. Yes, Michael loved the ocean's energy. It had brought him great fortune on that night.

As Michael breathed in the ocean scent and walked toward the dock and Blake's yacht, he hoped his choice of attire—cargo shorts, an old pair of deck shoes, a polo shirt and his busted watch was the right choice. He didn't know. He'd never been on a yacht.

He passed the restaurant, looked out toward the marina and stopped dead in his tracks as the yacht came into his sight. He could not believe his eyes. The yacht was stunning. It wasn't the typical, ultra contemporary vessel with wild elliptical curves that has come to define the modern yacht. No, this yacht recaptured the splendor, grace and charm of an era gone by. It was a down to the millimeter replication of a classic schooner bow and fantail-style stern motor-yacht that looked as if she just appeared straight out of the early 20th century. It was as if Michael had just stepped back in time. The vessel reminded him of the model ships his father used to build as a hobby when he was a little boy. Only this was no model. It was a 151-foot mega-yacht. He thought about his father and wished he were there to see it. He would have loved casting his eyes on this beauty. After realizing that he was staring with his mouth agape, Michael remembered that he had his cell phone in his pocket so he quickly pulled it out and snapped a couple pictures.

"She's a beauty, isn't she?" a voice came from behind.

"Sure is," Michael replied. His eyes remaining fixed on the vessel.

"Let's board her."

Michael turned to discover he was talking with Blake. He was instantly relieved when he noticed the millionaire was dressed in similar fashion, wearing plaid shorts and an expensive polo shirt.

He wore a Rolex watch on his right wrist and although Michael couldn't be certain, he would bet money that Blake's watch actually worked... that is, *if* he had money to bet.

While walking, Blake began to talk about his inspiration for the yacht, "I wanted her to bring me back to a time when people actually knew how to relax and enjoy the simple pleasures of yachting. She's quite true to the period with one notable exception. She's outfitted with the latest engineering, materials, systems and amenities available today."

As they came up to the vessel, Michael was in awe of the high quality craftsmanship of everything from the overall design down to the detail of the trail boards flanking the bow, which were adorned with gold leaf. Blake followed Michael's gaze and knew what he was admiring. "One man spent more than two hundred hours carving those trail boards." he explained, "I was planning to commission them, but the intricate detail I desired required more than what the machine was programmed to manufacture."

Blake stopped at the edge of the dock, one step away from boarding the yacht, and turned to face Michael, "Well?"

At first, Michael stood frozen, waiting for Blake to continue. Then he realized what the millionaire was waiting for. "Oh, I'm sorry." He said, pulling a folded up piece of paper out of his back pocket. "I came up with 285 names, but I thought of a few more on my way down here today."

Blake was pleased, but that was only half of the criteria, "And the CD's?" he asked.

"I listened to all twenty-five of them." Michael replied. "I really enjoyed them. I was hoping to purchase them from you."

The millionaire resisted his urge to smile. He didn't want to seem impressed by Michael's initiative, but he was. "Keep them," Blake said, "just pay it forward when the time is right."

"Are you sure?" Michael asked.

Blake didn't respond. He wouldn't have said it if he didn't mean it.

The millionaire boarded the yacht with Michael in tow. Once on the vessel, Blake passionately resumed sharing details about the yacht. "The mast is removable. I designed it that way for when the yacht transits beneath low bridges on inland waterways. My dream has been to cruise America's famous rivers, Intracoastal waterways and Great Lakes while making regular excursions to the Caribbean. It's something I couldn't do with my other yacht."

Other yacht, Michael thought, *I'm actually talking to a man who owns YACHTS.*

As expected, the ships interior was as impressive as her exterior and also reflected the 1920's. The walls were adorned with white painted panels and madrona burl paneling that was accented by ebony inlays and a brilliantly carved red-toned African wood molding. They were complemented by teak and sycamore soles in some places and cream-tone carpeting in others. The hardware and appliances were stainless steel and the insets and faucets were made of crystal. It was perfect, a piece of art. Blake continued talking about how the vessel came to fruition, "My wife and I have been planning this yacht in our minds for many years. She is the culmination of a lifetime of dreaming, planning and working," he said, as he completed the tour, "Isn't that right Captain Martin?"

"Yes Sir," the Captain replied.

Standing in the room, behind Michael was a distinguished, almost regal looking gray-haired man wearing formal Captain's attire. He stood erect like a military soldier preparing to salute and members of the crew and staff that was equally as notable flanked him.

"Michael, this is Captain Martin, his crew will be taking us out to sea today," the millionaire avowed.

"Hello," Michael greeted him, nodding his head once to acknowledge the Captain and his crew.

"Sir," the Captain replied, returning the gesture before redirecting his attention to the millionaire, "Mr. Easton, we are prepared to cast off at your request."

Michael tried his best to hide the fact that he was in awe of his immediate state of affairs. He wanted to jump out of his skin, have a mini-convulsion, and jump back in, but he stood as still as the yacht itself and waited for the millionaire to make the next move.

"The others will be boarding soon," Blake said, "We can depart as soon as they arrive."

"Very well Sir," the Captain replied, before he and his crew left the room so that the two men could continue their conversation in private.

"I asked you to come a few minutes early so we could have time to catch up." The millionaire motioned towards comfortable looking couches near the cabin windows, overlooking the water, "Have a seat."

They settled down in the cabin, sitting across from each other, slightly angling their bodies so they could look out towards the water. Both of them spoke in depth about recreational activities that each of them enjoyed before the conversation landed on the topic of business.

"So," Blake began, "tell me about your meeting."

"Well, it didn't go exactly the way I hoped it would," Michael admitted, "the truth is, only one person showed up."

"How many people did you invite?"

"Six," Michael said. He was clearly disappointed. He wondered why the system that had obviously worked for others, simply did not work for him.

"How many did you think would show?" Blake asked.

"Well, at least five. They're my friends. I don't know why they did this to me."

Michael's frustration was obvious.

"Did they tell you they were coming?" Blake questioned.

"They all said they would try and make it," Michael answered.

The millionaire knew this was the perfect moment to educate Michael by sharing a valuable principle that would serve him well in business. "Michael, most individuals approach business, and quite frankly life in general, with improper expectations. When our expectations are off, that is when we are most prone to get upset. In other words, the only way you'll ever get upset in this business is when something opposite of what you were expecting happens. Proper expectations are essential if you intend to make it in this industry. When our expectations are not aligned with proper actions, we encounter frustrations. I can clearly see that you are frustrated, so let me ask you a question. What would you say if a friend of yours called you up and said, 'Michael, I have ten thousand dollars in cash that I am giving away tonight at my house. You are the first person I've called and I would like to give it to you. Can you be here in an hour?'"

"I'd tell him that I'll be there in ten minutes." Michael replied.

"Exactly. You would assure him that you would be there. You wouldn't tell him that you would TRY and make it. Try, in this industry, means—I am not coming." Blake explained, "Now, one of two things needs to get fixed here. First, if you invited your prospect properly, but they do not show interest or act as if they are going to try to make it, you simply shouldn't expect them to show. This way, there would be no frustration. You are sifting and sorting, not begging or trying to talk someone into the business. You only need a few, and the sooner you move someone though your system, the sooner you can move through your list and find the right ones to build your team with."

Michael was listening intently.

Blake continued, "The second thing we must work on is the way you are communicating with people. It's important to invite people properly. This is called posture. I'll explain in a minute, but first, tell me what you said when you made the calls?"

"Well, I told them I just got involved with a business opportunity that I wanted to tell them about."

Blake cringed. Only one word escaped his mouth, "Wow."

"Michael, where on those CD's were you told to say things like 'got involved with' and 'business opportunity'?"

He wasn't told to use these words. They just seemed to make sense. They felt comfortable, which was something Michael craved since he was surprisingly uncomfortable making those calls in the first place. Even though he talked to these people regularly, it was about sports or family or home improvement type things. Michael had no problem calling one of his electrician friends and asking for advice when he was installing outdoor floodlights, but calling about a network marketing business was different. The way Michael looked at it, since he helped his buddy Ron put a new roof on his garage, the least Ron could have done was show up to see the business, especially given the fact that he said he would.

"I don't get it? How could the words I used be so wrong?" Michael asked.

"Michael, this business is so simple, it's hard."

The look of confusion on Michael's face was becoming familiar to Blake, so he continued, "Most people in this industry focus on what to say. They attend trainings, listen to audios and engage in conversation to try to figure out the magic words or phrases that are going to get them rich. Meanwhile, I have made millions in this industry learning what NOT to say. Through the years, I have come to realize that the prospecting message often becomes blurred because people use the wrong words or say too much, yet the masters have learned what not to say. The good news for you is, now you know at least six different things not to say. Don't worry Michael, I slipped up just the other day and said something I wished I wouldn't had. Even I'm still learning."

Michael began to wonder if he bit off more than he could chew. His initial thought was that all he would have to do is call people, invite them over, and sign them up. He neglected to take into consideration the process he had to go through before he made the decision to sign up. He thought this would be the right time to share a recent conversation he and Kristen had.

"My wife thinks it's harder to build the business in this area than it is in other places," Michael said.

"Michael, my business is currently in 17 countries and I heard that same thing said in every part of every one of those countries. It's simply not true." the millionaire replied. Blake was familiar with the thoughts that were running through Michael's mind. The millionaire had been in the game for far too long. "Along the lines of what we've been speaking about, let me give you some insight into the skill of posture. An understanding of this will set you apart from the masses in this industry."

Michael raised his left eyebrow and tipped his head slightly, "Posture?"

"Posture is how people receive you in terms of confidence and attitude. It's essential for you to understand that people decide whether or not they want to be in business with you by the way you handle yourself. Before you even mention the reason why you're calling, you have to project strength and posture."

"How do I do that?"

"It's actually a lot easier than you think. Based on my assessment of working with thousands of network marketers— some of whom have reached the highest levels, yet others can't get off the ground using the same simple recruiting system— posture really is communicated in this industry through three universal principles." The mentor held up three fingers and said, in his most serious tone, "Once you understand and master them, you'll be unstoppable. They are your *first impression*, your *ability to stay in control* and learning to *utilize the take away*."

Blake paused for a moment to let those three principles sink in. "Michael, there are accidental words that you used when you made those calls that produced a poor first impression. These words are so innocent that most people don't even realize they're saying them."

"What words?"

"For starters, the words *business opportunity*," Blake replied, "even if you are calling a friend who knows, likes and trusts you, once you say those words, his mind will immediately begin to close."

Michael was perplexed. "Why?"

"Put yourself in your friend's shoes for a moment. Over the years, he has probably heard the term business opportunity so much that it sends instantaneous messages to his brain, which causes an automatic defensive mechanism to kick in. The funny thing is he doesn't even know why he reacts this way. Maybe he doesn't even mean to, but he immediately begins to dismiss the notion that you may have something worth listening to because of the negative feelings that accompany these two words. This is usually a result of previous experiences. Whether it's infomercials that turned him off, an overly aggressive family member trying to sell the latest deal they're into, or the fact that he himself has tried four to five other business opportunities, whatever the reason, you simply don't want to compete with this."

"Wow, I never thought about it that way."

"One little twist on that phrase can make all the difference. Instead of using the words *business opportunity*, tell your prospects that you *have an idea* that you want to run by them. There are many other simple words you could use also, but the point is that most don't pay attention to what not to say. This type of simple change to a less confrontational word like 'idea' will increase your chances of accomplishing your goal, which is to move people through your system so you can build belief, and present your business."

Such a simple change, but Blake's logic made complete sense.

"Okay, I get it. You also mentioned the words 'got involved with.' Why was that wrong?" he asked.

"Those three words have an even worse effect on people. Think about ways in which you have heard those words used together in the past. Mary got involved with those kids that were expelled from school. Billy got involved with that guy who was selling *xyz*. Remember, it wasn't too long ago that hundreds of people got involved with the Bernie Madoff scam and lost their life savings. When you tell a prospect that you just got involved with something, their immediate thoughts go to something negative. When you use phrases such as 'got involved with', you're accidentally sending the signal that you're trying to get them involved in something too. As a result, they start running the opposite direction and don't even know why. Does that make sense?"

"Yes," Michael said, as he chuckled. It was almost as if Blake had been listening to his conversations with his prospects.

"Now, the last thing you said wrong was that you wanted to tell them about your business."

This confused Michael. How could he possibly tell anybody about his business if he wasn't supposed to actually *tell* anybody about his business?

"You lost me," he said.

"Michael, you're brand new. The ink hasn't even dried on your application yet. If you lead into the conversation stating that you want to tell someone about your business, then they are going to want to hear about it from you. The end result will be them making a decision based on what you say and you don't know enough about the business to have success doing this."

"So then, how do I get them information?"

"First, always think through everything you do as if you are training your newest member on how to build the business. This is called the 'duplication mindset'. Remember, it's not how good you are, it's how duplicable your methods are. You want to use your proven team system and provide information through multiple 3rd party exposures," Blake explained. "Use the scripts and always invite more people than you can fit in the space you have. The key is to maintain your posture and keep moving forward. You are sifting and sorting. Most people quit well before they've even given their business an honest start. Everything has a learning curve. Don't worry about last minute cancellations or no shows. You will definitely get some of them. Even at my wedding there were no shows, and we were serving free food and drinks."

The millionaire laughed. He realized Michael wasn't joining in. Studying the young man's body language, Blake was beginning to realize that his young mentee was still unclear on something. "You have a question."

"Yes, you referred to posture as a skill. I don't understand."

"Everything it takes to build this business can be learned, which makes it a skill. The key is to want it bad enough, do you?"

"Yes."

"Then let me give you a simple formula for success. If you master and apply this formula, you will change your life."

This was one of those moments Michael was anticipating. He loved simple things. Every time the millionaire gave him a key phrase or concept, he knew he was receiving the type of message he could easily understand and apply. This was one of those times.

Blake then said seven simple words, "Dream plus belief, times action, equals results."

There didn't seem to be much more of an explanation needed. Michael pulled a small pad and pen out of his pocket and wrote the following: $Dream + Belief \times Action = Results$.

From the corner of his eye, Michael noticed a couple boarding the yacht. They easily captured his full attention. There was an air about them that only financially successful people seemed to have. He could tell they were wealthy.

Blake turned to see what had captured Michael's attention. A smile appeared. It was clear that this was one of the couples the millionaire was expecting.

"Richard and Dawn Parker" Blake said, "They are the biggest failures in our industry from the state of Connecticut."

"Failures? They look like millionaires." Michael observed.

"They are," Blake acknowledged. "In fact, they are the top income earners in our company from that state."

"Then why would you call them failures?"

Blake peered into Michael's eyes, "Because they have heard more people say no than anyone else in Connecticut. They failed their way to massive success. They didn't base their strategy on who they thought was going to say yes or no, they based it on how many people they were willing to take through our system."

Michael understood the point Blake was making, but he still felt as if this couple must have had an advantage. They looked like they socialized with a different caliber of people than he did. Richard was tall and handsome and sported a neatly manicured moustache. Dawn had fiery red hair and blue eyes. She was elegant and classy. They complimented each other nicely.

Michael was convinced they must have been very successful before network marketing. His curiosity had gotten the better of him, "What did they do for work before this business?"

"Richard worked for a chemical company, and Dawn was a beautician."

As Blake finished his sentence, the couple entered the cabin. The millionaire approached and greeted them with a hug. They were obviously very close. After sharing a few quick pleasantries, Blake made formal introductions.

"Richard, Dawn, I'd like you both to meet Michael Harper. I knew his father. Michael just joined the team. I'm going to mentor him."

Richard reached out to shake Michael's hand, and in a pleasant manner said, "It's very nice to meet you, Michael."

"You too," Michael replied.

"I'm sure you already know this, but you're very lucky to be learning from Blake." Dawn added, "Somebody up there must like you."

"I'm beginning to think that myself," Michael replied.

She redirected her attention back to Blake, "How's that beautiful wife of yours?" Dawn asked.

"She's wonderful. The charity benefit is today so she couldn't make it, but she's excited to see everyone tonight. How was your retreat?"

"Wonderful." She stressed, "You were so right. It was exactly what we needed to bond with our new group. I can't wait to tell you about it."

"Hold that thought," Blake turned his attention to Richard, "Michael just had his first meeting. He had a hard time getting friends to come and look at the business, and a few who told him they would come, but were last minute cancellations. I was talking to him about posture. Before you even walked into the cabin you seemed to make an impression on him, Dawn and I are going to catch up, would you take a moment to talk with him about first impressions?"

"I'd be happy to," Richard said. He immediately turned his attention to Michael and began by asking the question, "What do you sell?"

Michael thought this was an odd question since Blake just explained that he was new to the business. "The same thing you do," He answered.

"No, I mean, what do you sell?" Richard repeated.

"Well..." Baffled, Michael began to rattle off the names of some of the core products his company had built its reputation on. Richard raised his hand, an obvious signal to bring an end to his answer.

"No Michael. That is what our company sells." He replied. "I want to know what *YOU* sell." Michael remained quite. He wasn't sure how to reply. Sternly, Richard said, "*YOU* sell *YOU*."

Before Michael could respond, Richard continued, "Do you know what a first impression is?" His words came out his mouth faster than Michael was used too. It was something that even took a native New Jerseyan by surprise.

"Blake started to talk about this a little, but I know he wanted to share more." Michael began. He knew they hadn't finished the conversation, and so he asked, "Does this have anything to do with how a person dresses?"

"No, I'm talking about the importance of making a great first impression with the people you are showing the business too. Let's continue where Blake left off. He's helped people, including my family, make millions by understanding what I'm about to share with you. Don't take this the wrong way Michael, but the people you are going to be talking with will not only be considering the company, they will also be considering whether or not they want to be in business with you. So the question is, would you get into business with you?"

"I understand what you're asking," Michael said, "but I don't think that was a factor because the people I invited all knew me for years." Michael rationalized.

"That doesn't matter. There are several unwritten laws when it comes to business. Let me explain the law of the first impression in regard to sales," Richard began. "This law gets violated more than any other. Simply put, the law states that the close begins in the first thirty seconds. Have you ever met someone that you knew you wanted to be in business with?"

"Yes," Michael replied. Blake was the first one who came to his mind, but he didn't verbalize it.

"That person has posture," Richard explained. "You immediately know a person who has posture when you meet them. They have an air about them. You know they are the type of person who is destined to accomplish what they set out to, and if you expect to succeed, then you must also have posture. For some, good posture comes naturally, but for the majority of us, it's learned. It's not about arrogance and it's certainly not about desperation. It's about confidence." He continued, "I don't want to disappoint you, but nobody is interested in buying your product. Every day, people are bombarded with thousands of advertisements where someone is trying to get one thing from them—their money. You have to be different. Don't sell products, sell lifestyle. Sell hope. Sell yourself as the person that is going to lead them in the direction of their dreams, then follow through."

"How can I do that when I haven't accomplished anything yet?" Michael wondered audibly.

"You'll never accomplish anything if you don't believe you can. Nothing happens by accident. You have to know where you are going and you can't call people and ask for permission to speak. People will never follow a person who is unsure of themselves. You have to be in control of the conversation. Do you think you can do that?"

"I'll try." Michael replied, sheepishly.

"You *try* sushi. You *try* on a pair of boots. When it comes to business, try is another word for fail." Richard rebuked. "Try is a word weak people use. Do you have a dictionary at home?"

Michael was caught off guard by the change in direction. "Yes," he replied.

"When you get home tonight," Richard directed, "take a black marker and cross out the word *try*. While you're at it, do the same to the words *can't* and *impossible*. As far as you're concerned, from this moment on, those words no longer exist. You are going to have to remove those words from your vocabulary."

"Okay," Michael consented.

"Now, back to the first impression," Richard said, reverting to the topic at hand. "When people in sales get nervous, they begin to ramble and end up saying things they shouldn't. If your prospects don't have the right information, they'll make their entire decision based on what you say and how you act. You have to stay in control of the conversation and strategically lead it where you want it to go. The words that come out of your mouth are very important," he advised.

Michael knew he was receiving great information. Blake was just stressing the same message before Richard even entered the cabin. He didn't want to risk the chance of forgetting any of it, so he pulled out his small pad and jotted down Richard's advice.

Michael could feel his forearm starting to tighten as he wrote as fast as he could. All the while, Blake continued to greet more guests. Suddenly, unexpectedly, Richard asked, "Do you like lemonade?"

He stopped writing and looked up. Unsure if he heard the question right he asked, "Do what?"

"Lemonade? Do you like it?" he repeated.

"Oh, yes, I do."

Richard looked over at two crewmembers standing nearby, "Would you be kind enough to bring us two lemonades," he said. One of them nodded his head and quickly left the room.

Michael laughed—inside, of course.

"Don't take the fact that no one showed up for your meeting personally. To be honest, you shouldn't even call it a meeting. No one wants to come home from work and then go off to a meeting." Richard continued, "There is one simple thing you can do to prevent a no show from happening again."

"What's that?" Michael asked.

Before Richard could answer, Blake stepped into the center of the room and announced, "Captain Martin, we're all here."

The Captain nodded and the crew went to work instantly. After a swift cast off, the vessel headed out to sea. Michael looked around. There were three couples and one single male on the yacht with him and Blake. Each person looked as impressive as the couple from Connecticut did. He couldn't help but to feel like a Little League baseball player who just snuck into a MLB all-star locker room. The single male was about 6'1" with a muscular frame and looked very familiar. Michael figured he must just resemble someone he had met before. After all, how could he possibly know another person on this yacht? When he turned back to hear the answer to his question, Richard was already talking with one of the other couples. He would have to wait to find out what that one simple thing was.

Say Less to More

Blake AND HIS GUESTS were standing in the center of the cabin, when he said, "I couldn't imagine sharing this moment with a more deserving group of friends."

Although this may not exactly be *The Majestic Treasure's* official maiden voyage, it was her official maiden test run out to sea. Blake chose to share this special experience with these people. How Michael made the list was a mystery to him, but he certainly wasn't going to complain.

Blake lifted his glass to make a toast, "I assume everyone has a drink?"

Michael was happy that a crewmember just handed him a glass of pink lemonade. As everyone raised their glasses, Michael followed suit. He initially wondered what everyone else was drinking, but quickly realized that this was a non-alcohol voyage.

With glasses raised, Blake gave his toast, "There are good ships, and there are wood ships, the ships that sail the sea. But the best ships are friendships, and may they always be."

"Cheers," Richard said, before he and the others completed the toast.

"I'm sure you're all wondering who this young man is," Blake said, referring to Michael. All eyes fell upon him, which would make him uncomfortable in any situation, especially this particular one, where he had that glass of pink lemonade pressed against his lips. He stood, frozen, waiting for Blake to continue, "I'd like to take a moment to introduce you to someone from my old neighborhood and one of our newest members whom I am going to be taking under my wing. His name is Michael Harper."

The group said hello to Michael. He reciprocated.

"Welcome to the team," said the man who looked familiar. Even his voice sounded familiar.

Who is that? He wondered, before saying, "Thank you."

The guests turned toward each other to begin mingling. Michael was eager to continue his conversation with Richard.

What was that one simple thing? He wondered.

He stood near Richard, waiting to get his attention, but Blake approached with another couple who he wanted to introduce to Michael. The couple looked to be in their fifties. The male was shorter than he was, with neatly trimmed salt and pepper hair. She was a lovely woman with an infectious smile. They were Steve and Mary Morrison, from Florida. At Blake's request, they shared their story with Michael.

Steve was a real estate investor and developer. Mary was a successful entrepreneur who, at one time, owned three businesses. Even before network marketing, they appeared to have it all. The problem was they also had the debt and the stress that came from having to juggle their many business ventures. The couple initially joined network marketing because they believed they could earn the type of income they had become accustomed too, without having to stress over every intricate detail that came with their professions—things like employee problems and high overhead.

Years earlier, Steve was convinced that he had his eyes on the light at the end of the tunnel. After years of stress, however, he came to the realization that the light he was looking at was a freight train coming directly at him. In the conversation Steve and Mary had with Michael, they shared their story and explained how they hoped network marketing would be the answer they were looking for... It was.

Michael only wished his wife, who had chosen to stay home with the baby that morning, was with him to hear their story. During their conversation, Blake again mentioned that Michael had just experienced a bad first meeting.

"Steve and Mary are experts on having bad meetings." Blake said, it was obviously an inside joke. "They learned the hard way how to stay in control of a conversation."

Blake then asked the couple to share some of their wisdom. They were happy to oblige.

"Michael, I have always believed that if a person has a hard time getting people to come and look at the business, it's usually a result of poor posture," Steve said. "Of the people you called, how many sincerely wanted to know more about the business?"

Michael took a moment to ponder the question before realizing that none of the people he talked with expressed much interest at all. His one friend showed up, but he really didn't seem open-minded.

"To be honest, none of them did." He reluctantly shared.

"Then you must be doing or saying something wrong. People don't just turn away from an opportunity unless they think they know what it is. You have to stop trying to explain the business over the phone."

"How did you know I did that?" he asked.

"Everyone does that." Steve answered. Turning to his wife, he added, "Right sweetheart?"

Mary smiled and added, "The Bible tells the story of how Sampson slayed one thousand Philistines with the jawbone of an ass. My husband used that same weapon to blow out just as many prospects when we started."

They all laughed.

"She's right Michael. I can speak from experience. Getting me to open my mouth about this business was never the problem. My problem was learning when to keep my mouth shut." Steve explained, "If you walk up to a friend you hadn't seen in a year, he isn't thinking that you are in one of those pyramid things. So, if two minutes into your conversation he says he isn't interested in something like this, it's the words you are using and the way you are carrying yourself that would make him think that way. What I'm trying to say is, ninety percent of all sales success is a result of your ability to stay in control of a conversation."

Michael began taking notes again. He started by writing down the last sentence that Steve had just said to him.

"Remember this." Steve continued, "Conversation before presentation always ends in failure! Just about anything you would say to a prospect before they see your presentation will cause you problems."

Michael cut him off, "So, what should I say?"

"Say less to more people." Steve replied, "Don't ever disregard the fact that most people lose control of the conversation the moment their prospect begins to ask questions. This is where the sale is almost always lost."

Michael quickly scanned his memory and realized that all of his close friends had asked him what it was before they took the time to look at the presentation. Based on what he had just learned, his conversations definitely went into more detail than they should have.

"When someone asks you questions, how do you answer them?" Michael asked.

"There are two primary ways to answer questions. If you master them, you're going to produce much greater results. The first is to answer a question with a question." Steve explained.

"I'm not sure I understand."

"Let me give you an example," Steve offered, "If you call Bob and he asks if what you are sharing with him has anything to do with sales, you could answer with the question, 'Why, do you like sales?' The interesting thing about that last question is, whether Bob answers yes or no, you can reply with, 'Then you're going to love this,' and move on. If he likes sales, *great* he can sell all he wants, if not, *great* he can benefit from our products. If he's interested in making money, he will have the opportunity to build a team and benefit from the sales of others. Either way, it's a win/win question."

"That's great," Michael admitted. "What's the second way to answer questions?"

"My favorite way to answer my prospects questions is by bringing them through our system. In other words, every question your prospect asks is a reason to move them into the next step. If they haven't seen the presentation, but ask you how much it costs to join, you should answer by telling them that you have a brief video that will cover that question and provide additional details. Then you can suggest a time when the two of you can meet so you can get all of his questions answered. You do this by showing them your presentation."

"So, you never let them lead the conversation where they want it to go?" Michael concluded.

"Never," Steve said.

"Blake also said something about the take away. What did he mean by that?" Michael asked.

The timing of his question could not have been better, as the words left his mouth, another guest, Andrew Pearle, approached.

"This is the man you want to talk with." Steve said, "Andrew is king of the take away."

Without hesitation, Andrew began with, "There is no other technique in sales that displays your level of posture better than the take away."

Michael immediately recognized this man's voice from one of the CD's he had listened to. Andrew Pearle was a Navy Seal who, after his time in the service, went on to be a successful insurance salesman. He was looking for a way to diversify when someone called and asked if he had time to look over a business idea with him. Andrew, being the kind of guy who was always available to help a friend, willingly went to a presentation. His friend, ironically, never did much with the business, but Andrew did. The rest, as they say, was history. Andrew was a terrific speaker as was his wife, Kathy, who built her own networking business to a high level as a single mother before they met at a seminar, began dating and fell in love.

As Michael was writing the words "take away" on his pad, Andrew asked, "Wouldn't you agree that people want what they can't have?"

The question instantly caused Michael to think back to when he was in a freshman in high school. There was a quiet girl named Jenny who liked him, but he wasn't sure how he felt about her. Until, of course, she began dating one of his friends and became popular. As soon as Michael found out she was no longer available, he couldn't get her out of his mind. It was a feeling he had never forgotten, "Yes, as a matter of fact, I would agree."

"Michael, I know we are just getting to know each other, but let me tell you this. In almost every scenario of building your team you will have to utilize the take away in order to maintain your posture. If you're around Blake Easton very much, you'll understand that he absolutely has some of the best people skills you will ever witness, but make no mistake about it, he doesn't chase anyone. He takes it away. This is why people chase him down to be in business with him.

"If you ever find yourself trying to convince people to be interested in your business, take a step back and say, 'this may not be for you, or you may or may not be interested, but if you're open, I'll get you the facts so that you can make an intelligent decision.' Then, move to the next step of the system and book the appointment. Remember, *conversation* before *presentation* always ends in failure.

"It took me a little while to get comfortable utilizing the take away, but it works. Now, I wouldn't do it any other way. By the way, this is not about being rude or obnoxious, but when you give people permission to say *no*, they feel less threatened and are more comfortable letting you move forward."

"I like that," Michael admitted.

"Every time you decide that it's in your best interest to take it away from a prospect, you are telling yourself that this prospect may, or may not, deserve your time. This elevates your self-esteem, which elevates your posture, which, in turn, will elevate your closing ratio. Makes sense, doesn't it?" Andrew asked, nodding his head as if he was providing Michael with the answer.

"Yes."

Michael looked down at his half-empty glass of lemonade, which sat on the table nearby. The pink liquid reminded him that he never received his answer from Richard, about the one simple thing he could do to prevent a no show from happening again. He looked around the room, but the man was nowhere in sight. He was curious what that one thing was, but he was also thrilled to learn about the importance of the first impression and how to stay in control of a conversation. He would also certainly use the take away when the time was right. Michael was about to ask a question when he felt a hand on his shoulder. It was Blake's.

"Have you learned anything?" the millionaire asked.

He had. Michael had come to an obvious conclusion, "This thing is all about posture, isn't it?"

"You got it," Blake answered, "The people you just talked with make more money than most because they treated network marketing as a profession instead of an opportunity. You will become a master networker once you develop true posture."

Michael continued to scribble notes on his little pad.

"I learned a lot of great things," he said.

"Have you met everyone?" Blake asked.

"Not everyone," Michael replied. He scanned the room and fixed his eyes on the man with the familiar face. He was younger than the others, perhaps only a year or two older than Michael was. "That guy over there looks so familiar."

"Who does, Brad?"

"His name is Brad?" Even that sounded familiar. *How do I know him?* Michael thought.

"He was the running back for the Dallas Cowboys." Blake replied.

Michael's mouth dropped. "That's Brad Sharples?!"

Blake nodded.

"He was an all pro, and Super Bowl MVP, the same year he…" Michael stopped.

"Knocked the Giants out of the playoffs by scoring a touchdown in overtime," Blake finished.

"Yes."

"Well, we can forgive him for that. After all, the Giants had a chance to acquire him first, but they passed him up. I'd say they regretted it. At least on that day they did. Do you want to meet him?"

"I'm not sure. I think I lost forty bucks on that game." Michael joked, "Of course, I want to meet him."

Blake brought the two together and introduced them. Some of Brad's football stories captivated Michael, but he was mostly interested in hearing the ex-athlete's reasons for building his networking business. Brad had made a lot of money as a football player, but his pro career lasted less than eight years.

After football, Brad had tried several business ventures, but lost money on most of them. However, the biggest hit he took came when he found out that his manager had stolen the bulk of his earnings before disappearing a few years ago. When a friend approached Brad about this business, he did not want to do it, but he liked the product and was impressed with the compensation plan.

"I used to work out six hours a day," Brad shared. "Some days I did one thousand reps of squats. I didn't want to do that either, but it was one small part of what I needed to do if I wanted to become a running back in the NFL. Success is achieved in the weight room and the practice field. What people see on the football field is the results of what athletes do—day in and day out—when nobody is watching. That's where champions are made."

Michael wrote down that last sentence. He thought about that 67-yard touchdown run in overtime that took his Giants out of the playoffs years earlier, and for the first time, he was happy the game ended the way it did.

Brad had obviously paid his dues, and that same work ethic he developed as an all-pro athlete, carried him to the top of the network marketing industry as well.

"C'mon buddy," Blake said, waving Michael into another room, "Let's order lunch and talk about your next move."

The Only Difference

MICHAEL GAZED OUT at the incessant sea, "I was invited on a fishing trip once," he said.

"How was it?" Blake asked.

"I don't know. I didn't go." He answered, with a hint of disappointment in his tone. "I guess I thought I'd get seasick, or something."

"Do you feel seasick now?"

"Not at all. I'm so happy I'm here right now."

"You never know how you will respond to a new experience until you try it," Blake explained.

Michael knew this was another truth that he wished he had realized years ago. So many times he thought he knew how he was going to react to a situation. There were times when he would rationalize why he wouldn't want to go on a certain vacation or try a new experience. The only one he was hurting was himself, by not trying something new. At least he was still young enough to change his way of thinking, and thankfully, he was standing next to a man who could help him make that change.

"I learned so much today, Blake. Thank you for inviting me."

"Do you feel you understand posture now?"

"Yes, and I know it is a skill that I will consciously be looking to develop."

"Good. Because if you apply that formula we spoke of earlier and add posture into the mix, you will build a massive team."

Michael turned to the page in his pad where he scribbled, *Dreams + Belief x Action = Results* and jotted down the word *posture* next to it. "Is this all it really takes to do this?" he asked.

"Not completely," Blake answered, "building a business and holding it together are two completely different things. Yes, it takes skill to build a business, but it takes character to keep it together."

"Do you mean… honesty?"

"Well, yes, for starters, but it's more than just that." Blake explained, "It's about dependability, which means doing the things you said you would do long after the mood you said it in has passed."

"That's a great definition." Michael said.

"Thank you. I heard it on a CD." Blake said with a smile.

"So, what should I do now?" Michael asked.

"Schedule another meeting." Blake immediately replied.

The thought didn't excite Michael.

Blake continued, "Your rearview mirror is smaller than your windshield for a reason. If you let your past experiences get in the way of the present, you'll end up losing your future. You had a bad first meeting and a handful of no shows, big deal. Every one of the leaders you just met had no shows. Schedule another meeting," he repeated, "Only this time invite more people, maintain your posture and use our proven system."

Michael listened intently. "Should I re-invite my friends who didn't come last week?" he asked.

"Your job isn't to show your business to your five closest friends and hope for the best. Your job is to sift and sort through as many people as you can to see whose time is now. Sales, is a numbers game." Blake stressed, "And, you are doing more than just selling a product. You are offering people a chance at a better life. Think about all the people you went to high school with, the people who attended your wedding, your coworkers, the people at your church, your gym, your bakery, the guy who puts gas in your car. All those people whose names you put down on your list. Don't you care about them?"

"Yes, but every time I think about making a call to someone I haven't talked with in a while, I start to stress out," Michael shared. He didn't expect Blake's response.

"Why are you being selfish?" the millionaire asked. "You believe this business can change your life for the better, don't you?"

"Yes."

"Then why wouldn't you want others to have that opportunity?"

Michael reflected on what Blake had just said. "You're right."

"Don't complicate it Michael. A gift is only a gift if you are willing to share it with others."

"I understand. I'll call everyone on my list. Even people who I think wouldn't be interested?" he said.

"Don't prejudge people. Anyone can cut an apple and count how many seeds are in it, but no one can tell you how many apples will come from one good seed."

An expression of enlightenment came across Michael's face. "That makes complete sense."

"Now, I know you are going to have another home meeting, and that's the best way to get started, but I also want you to understand the importance of one-on-ones." Blake said.

"They talked a lot about one-on-one's on the CD's you gave me."

"That's because no one has ever reached significance in our industry without doing them."

"Why is that?" Michael asked.

"It's a whole lot easier to do ten one-on-one meetings than it is to have ten people come to your house." The millionaire explained, "Imagine the average person coming home from a long day at work. He heats up some dinner, takes a shower, and sits down in front of the television to relax for a minute. Only, a minute turns into an hour and he is so comfortable, the last thing he wants to do is get up, get dressed, and leave his home. Again, I'm talking about average people, but there are plenty of average people who have seeds of greatness within them."

"I just have to help them realize it," Michael finished.

"That's right, and people are less likely to cancel a meeting in their own home then they are yours. Also, one-on-ones give you the opportunity to place all of your attention on the person or couple you are talking with, instead of a roomful of people."

"True," Michael acknowledged.

A crewmember that had been standing near the door waiting for a break in the conversation leaned forward and announced, "Sir, lunch is prepared."

"Wonderful," Blake replied. "I'm starving."

Michael was delighted when a member of the kitchen staff brought two perfectly cooked, juicy pieces of filet mignon with sides of garlic mashed potatoes and asparagus.

"I hope you're not a vegetarian," the millionaire cautioned.

"Heck no," Michael replied, "I think vegetarian is really just an old Indian word for 'bad hunter.'"

Blake laughed vigorously. He didn't expect the comment. "I have to remember that one," the millionaire said. Michael was happy that he could amuse his host.

After their spectacular gourmet lunch, Michael and Blake stepped out onto the deck and walked toward the bow. Michael couldn't help but to realize that the yacht, which looked so big when docked, was not very large compared to the vastness of the sea. The ocean was mesmerizing, like an endless field of space with soft white edges. It was alive and constant. The swells appeared to move in slow motion as if the slightest breeze pushed them. The rhythm was hypnotic. The air smelled like salt and the ocean appeared heavy but graceful at the same time. *How could I describe this to people?* Before he could answer his own question, Blake asked him another.

"Michael, what was the last educational book you've read?"

"Educational? Wow, I'd have to think back to high school."

"I don't mean textbook." Blake rectified, "Have you ever heard the term 'personal growth?'"

After contemplating the question, "Yes, a few of the speakers on the CD's mentioned it."

"'Personal growth' is essential to a person's success, regardless of which profession they choose. You will never become the person of character like we discussed earlier if you are not consistently learning and changing. I once heard it said that you will be the same person in five years as you are today except for the people you meet, the books you read and the people you associate with. Consider the fact that millions of people have lived on this earth before you and I. There's no problem that you will encounter in life that someone else had not already concurred and written about. You can find the answer to most of life's questions in books."

"I never thought of it that way," Michael admitted, "What books would you suggest I read?"

"For starters, I would strongly recommend the two books we spoke about in my office. The first is Dale Carnegie's *How to*

Win Friends and Influence People, which will teach you how to effectively interact with others. Most people are unaware of the fact that the majority of the challenges they will have in business will be a direct result of a lack of people skills."

Since this was the second time Blake had mentioned this book. Michael felt a bit foolish that he did not pick up a copy yet. He wasn't going to make this mistake a second time.

"The other book is *Think and Grow Rich*," Blake said.

"What can I learn from that one?" Michael asked.

"That book will make you aware of the fact that everything we achieve and all that we fail to achieve is the direct result of our own thoughts. I was once asked what the most important lesson of my life was. I responded by saying that the biggest lesson I have ever learned is the astounding importance of what we think. Simply put, your thoughts make you what you are. By changing your thoughts, you can change your life. The book, *Think and Grow Rich* was written with that principle in mind."

Blake placed his hands on the railing and looked out toward the sea. "Every outcome in your life is a mirror reflection of your inner self. People like to make excuses for their failures. Some blame the economy, or the government, or corporate America. Others blame broken homes, lower social standings, or lack of education, but the person they should be blaming is the one in the mirror. There are people in this world who have overcome all of those excuses and their net worth is ten, even a hundred times your net worth, and mine too."

Michael wrinkled his forehead, "That's hard to believe," he said taking into consideration everything that Blake owns.

"It's true." The millionaire continued, "One has to ask the question, why? Why is it that you live in the same time, offer the same products, yet, get paid from the same commission plan and some people earn a million dollars a year while others only earn a couple hundred?" after a dramatic pause, he said, "The ONLY difference is YOU."

Michael wrote those five words down.

"It starts with changing the way you think. The day I made the decision to turn off the television and replace the junk they show on the news with words from books that were written by the most successful achievers in the world was the most liberating day of my life."

"You don't watch television?"

"Of course I do. I like a good game just like the next guy, but I'm very careful about what I allow to go into my mind." Blake held up the glass Michael had been drinking from. It was nearly empty, with just a drop of pink lemonade inside. "Your mind is like this empty glass." He said, "It will hold whatever you put into it. What you fill it with is what you become. The good news is, as dirty as this water may be when you start, to clear it up all you have to do is continuously flush it with clear water. That is how a personal growth program works and make no mistake about it, this will be essential if you intend to succeed."

"Everything you're saying makes sense," Michael validated, "This should all be taught in our school systems."

"I agree, but our school systems focus on formal education. Formal education will make you a living, but self-education will make you a fortune. A strong personal growth program will help you acquire more than just money. Self-improvement impacts everything. How you are as a husband. A father. A leader. It will teach you how to respect others and how to enjoy and love life."

"You must be so proud," Michael said.

"Why's that?" Blake asked.

"You're a self-made person. I mean, you dropped out of high school," Michael stressed, "and look at where you are today."

The millionaire held Michaels eyes for a long moment, then said, "Everyone's a self-made person Michael, but only the successful ones are willing to admit it. The Declaration of Independence states that all men are created equal, what happens after that, is a personal choice."

Michael was more impressed with Blake's wisdom than he was with the millionaire's yacht. He took a deep breath and celebrated the fact that he was receiving a first class education. He was proud of himself for making the effort to reach out to Blake, and he was thankful for the opportunity he had his hands on. He was excited and he knew he was going to lose sleep again tonight, but this time it wouldn't be due to stress. This time it would be a result of his excitement. He was eager to get back home and make calls.

"I learned so much from you and your friends today, Blake. I just hope I say the right things when I talk to my prospects."

"Remember, Michael, most new networkers spend all their time trying to figure out what to say. Instead, take a lesson from the people you had just spoken with. They've learned what *not* to say." Blake said, recapping the conversations that Michael and the top money earners in the other room just had.

"Character and skills," Michael said, summarizing his lesson by repeating the two things needed to build a successful business.

"Do you think you have what it takes?" Blake asked.

"I would have to say yes. If skills can be learned, I can learn them. If character can be developed, I can develop it. I suppose it all depends on whether or not my dream is big enough."

Blake was pleased with Michael's response. This was evident by the way the millionaire looked at him.

Michael couldn't go back and start a new beginning, but he could start now and make a new ending. He was beginning to believe—really believe—that he could achieve financial success. Still, he wondered aloud, "How do I instill belief in others?"

"I believe this business, and every great business in America for that matter, was built by one satisfied customer sharing their experience with another," Blake explained. "Don't underestimate the power of a testimony. If a person is willing to hear more about what you are doing, don't tell them everything you think you know about the business," Blake warned, "Instead, focus on providing them with multiple exposures. After meeting the people you just did and listening to what they just had to say, do you believe in this business more or less?" Blake asked.

"More."

"Of course," Blake said, "That's because you were listening to successful people who were passionate about the business. Passion is contagious. When you talk with someone on the phone, or in person, and they are interested in hearing more about the business, use third party credibility to build your prospects belief. You can do this over the phone, or by utilizing tools like online video's or CD's."

"How do I know when they are willing to hear more?"

"After you do something long enough, you develop an instinct, but the bottom line is if they express interest and haven't signed up or taken action, they need another exposure, and you just have to keep moving them in the right direction."

"It all seems so easy for you," Michael said. "If you want something you just go out and get it. It must be nice to be fearless. I wish I had the courage to be more like you."

"Courage isn't the absence of fear, it's the management of fear and sometimes courage is subtle. Like that quiet voice at the end of the day that says, tomorrow, I'll try again. You have to be willing to go day after day, until you achieve your goals. Set a thirty day goal for yourself. A game plan, if you will. When a person does a specific activity for thirty consecutive days it becomes a habit. You get to make your own habits, then, your habits get to make you. You just have to be consistent," Blake stated.

"Before you became successful, did you ever think about giving up?" Michael asked.

"Absolutely," Blake quickly admitted.

"How can that be," Michael questioned, "You have so much drive, and talent."

"Drive, yes, but talent in and of itself is overrated. I would rather work with a person who is tenacious than one who is just talented. Give me a person who is willing to take risks, not one who wants to remain in his comfort zone. In order to succeed, a person has to continuously step away from familiarity and towards their dreams. You can't discover new worlds unless you leave the port of familiar shores."

Michael looked out at the beautiful endless ocean and drew a deep breath. He couldn't tell where the water stopped and the sky began because he could hardly distinguish the edges. "You got that right," he whispered.

After their private counseling session, Blake and Michael regrouped with the others. Michael was a sponge, absorbing the nuggets of wisdom he was privileged to be receiving. When he came face-to-face with Richard, he was excited to finally hear the answer he had been waiting for.

"I have been wondering all day what that one simple thing is that I could do to prevent a no show from happening again."

Richard laughed. "I was hoping you asked me that," he admitted, "the answer is simple… Once you learn to harness the power of curiosity, you'll be able to maintain your prospects level of enthusiasm. If you do that, people will want what you have because they don't know what you have."

No further explanation was needed. Michael instantly realized that Richard had demonstrated the power of curiosity first hand by not answering his question right away. It was a brilliant way to make a point.

The *Majestic Treasure* returned to the marina after several hours at sea. Michael was inspired and ready to take action. The cruise was relaxing on the body and the education he received was priceless. His day with the millionaire exceeded all expectations and as a result, he felt a renewed commitment.

They exited the vessel, walked down the dock and through the parking lot, and stopped at Blake's Mercedes. Michael watched as the industry leaders that he had just shared the day with drove off in their expensive cars.

"Blake, I can't thank you enough for inviting me on your beautiful yacht. It was the opportunity of a lifetime. You can't imagine how much this meant to me."

They shook hands, "You're welcome, Michael." Digging into his pocket, Blake pulled out his keys and unlocked his door. Before entering his car, he asked, "If I remember correctly, you were a runner in high school, weren't you?"

"Yes, cross-country," Michael said with a smile, "You have a good memory."

"When you used to run long distances, and your legs started burning, do you remember that little voice that would tell you that you're too tired and the pain is too much? The one that would beg you to stop?"

"I remember that voice all too well," Michael answered.

"What did you do when you heard it in the middle of a race?"

"I kept running."

"Exactly," Blake replied, knowing this was a lesson Michael would never forget. "That's the same voice that will tell you to quit when anything becomes difficult in your life. If you can learn to defeat that voice, you can concur and accomplish anything."

The lesson was complete. Blake patted Michael on the shoulder before settling into the driver's seat of his car. Michael turned and began to walk toward his own vehicle. He opened the door to his car when Blake pulled up next to him with his window rolled down. "Do you remember how to get to my house?" He asked.

"Yes." Michael answered.

"Why don't you and Kristen stop by and have dinner with us two weeks from today? I want to introduce our better halves to each other and hear about your progress."

Michael cringed slightly, enough for Blake notice. Instead of waiting for the question, he blurted out, "Kristen's belief level is not quite there yet."

"Don't worry about that," Blake said, "We can have a nice dinner together, and then, you and I can step away and talk business."

That sounded reasonable to Michael, "We'll be there."

Blake reached up and handed Michael a CD.

"What's this?" Michael asked.

"Something to help you make calls," the millionaire answered.

Michael looked at the CD cover and realized he didn't even have to ask the question. It was titled, *Overcoming Your Fear of the Phone.*

"Be sure to bring your son. My wife has a soft spot for babies," Blake added, before driving off. Michael stood there dumbfounded momentarily, wondering why Blake was so willing to help.

Instead of questioning it, he knew he had to go and have a successful home meeting and a productive two weeks with his business. Now, he was accountable to someone and he didn't want to look foolish.

14

Do What You Fear

KRISTEN ONCE ASKED, about three or four months ago, "Why don't you ever come home excited? Aren't you happy to see us?" She was referring to the way Michael would enter the house. No smile. Without that gleam in his eye that she had seen earlier in their relationship.

"It's not you. It's just work," he answered.

His response didn't justify his actions, but it was the truth—partially, anyway. Yes, Michael found it frustrating to listen to his coworkers complain about everything. He also found it to be very stressful having to work for a man that demanded so much and never showed any appreciation. Truthfully, it was more than that. It was how the daily grind affected him in such a negative way that it began sucking the life out of him.

The traffic. The worn-out uniform. The clique that he was not a part of. The unfulfilling work he was assigned to do at the dead-end job. Then more traffic, and all for what... a paycheck that didn't meet his family's needs. That, in a nutshell, was his workday. The main reason behind his downheartedness went deeper than that. Michael had started to believe the voices of others. He spent so much time listening to negative people, negative radio personalities, and doom-and-gloom newscasters that he was starting to believe their words about how external circumstances were making it impossible for him to achieve anything of significance. Michael had lost his ability to dream the way he did as a boy.

On his way home from the yacht, Michael felt different. He felt that young, nine-year-old boy inside start to come alive again, the boy who once had a dream of being a sandcastle building champion—so much so that at the age of nine, his father bought him several books on the subject, built a six foot wide sand box in his yard, and filled it with sand from the beach. Michael would go out in the yard after his homework and, with a pitcher of water and a few buckets, practice making castles and objects using the techniques described in the books. When his father heard about a sandcastle building contest that was happening in Seaside Heights that summer, he promised Michael he would bring him down to watch and maybe even enter him in the youth novice category.

Michael spent the next two weeks dreaming of winning that contest, the way only a nine-year-old boy would. On the morning of the contest, his father received a call. It was his boss. There was an emergency and his father was the unlucky person who had picked up the phone. He was told he had no choice but to come in for two hours. Michael's father promised he would take him as soon as he did what they needed him to do at work, and he fulfilled that promise. However, by the time they reached the shore, the contest had already ended, and even though the weather reports called for a 10% chance of rain, it started drizzling before they stepped out of the car.

Michael and his father rushed from castle to castle, trying to see each work of art before the rain melted them away. The day was not as thrilling as Michael had envisioned it to be. Within a couple of weeks, he had lost his enthusiasm about becoming a sandcastle building champion. As the years went by, he hardly ever played in the box his father built, even though it sat in his yard for many years.

Yes, his circumstances at work and being surrounded by negative people all day long were one of the main reasons why Michael lost his ability to dream the way he did as that young boy in his new sandbox. As he grew older, he found it more and more difficult to leave his problems where they belonged—at work.

After spending a day on the yacht with such positive people, his entrance into his home on this day was quite different. The first thing Michael did when he saw his wife was hug and kiss her the way he used to when they were dating. At first, she was taken back, but she welcomed the passionate embrace she once took for granted, and returned the gesture.

"How was it?" she asked.

Michael began to tell Kristen about his day with Blake and the others. He was talking quickly, like Richard, his new friend from Connecticut. It was so out of character for him that Kristen found it to be cute and began to laugh. She loved to see him so excited, like he used to be when they first met.

Michael shuffled through a kitchen drawer and found a thick black permanent marker, "Where's our dictionary," he asked.

Kristen thought the request was odd, but she opened another drawer and pulled one out. Michael quickly flew through the pages until he came up to the word *can't*. He took the cap off the marker and drew a thick line over the word and its definition.

"What on earth are you doing?" she questioned.

"I'm crossing out the word *can't*," he answered. "As far as I'm concerned, from this day forward, that word no longer exists." He did the same with the words *impossible* and *try,* as he explained his reasoning, at light speed. "My entire life I talked myself out of success. I never realized it until today. Do you know that the words you use are important? I will never again use the words, *can't*, *try* or *impossible*. My son will never know these words exist." He was talking faster than Kristen could keep up. She was doing everything she could to keep from laughing at his nearly incoherent babbling.

"We need to buy the books, *How to Win Friends and Influence People* and *Think and Grow Rich*. By the way, we're going to have dinner with the Easton's in two weeks. Don't get a babysitter, Laura loves babies. Did you eat? I'm not hungry. Do we have any other dictionaries in the house?"

Later that night, after reliving every conversation he had on the yacht, Kristen helped Michael expand their names list. She was resistant at first, but after hearing how enthusiastic her husband had become, she caught his energy and began to write down names of people she knew using the Memory Jogger.

By taking Blake's advice about not pre-judging, they were able to come up with another 150 names. Kristen actually enjoyed going through various professions that were listed in alphabetical order and answering the questions, *who do we know that's an accountant, who do we know that works in a bank, who do we know that's a carpenter*? They continued that technique until the last profession, which was zookeeper.

"Really?" Kristen said sarcastically, "Zookeeper?"

They laughed. Ironically, it made them think of a woman who ran a petting zoo about an hour away from their house. They placed her name on the list.

The next day, Michael purchased business building supplies that Blake and his up-line partners recommended to better prepare him for his upcoming meeting. He understood that every profession had tools. Just as a carpenter uses a hammer to put nails in wood and a drill to make holes, he needed tools to show his business and materials to hand out to prospects so he could follow-up correctly. After spending the day on the ocean in Blake's yacht and gaining some insight as to how wealthy people think, he was no longer reluctant to invest in his business. Michael was beginning to think like a businessman. One who knew he was in a position to win.

Still, even with the new outlook, Michael had a hard time preparing to do the thing that scared him the most... make phone calls. He had rehearsed his call script so much that he had committed every word to memory, but that didn't make the task any less frightening for him. The way the conversations played out in his mind, were not the way they were going to play out when there was a person on the opposite end of the phone. Three times he picked up the phone to make calls to invite people to meetings he had scheduled at his house, and three times he put it back down.

Then he remembered. Blake had given him a CD to help overcome the fear of the phone. Michael hurried out to his garage and found that CD in the front seat of his car. He put it in his player and listened to the speaker tell a crowd about what she went through while making her first call.

"I remember sitting down at my desk getting ready to make my first call," she said, "I had my list, my script and a cup of coffee. I was ready to go. The only problem was... my phone was gone. It just vanished, and it was a beautiful phone too. A princess phone that I had since I was teenager, it was passed down from my grandmother, to my mother, and now to me, and it was gone – and in its place was a large, hairy, black phone, with fangs—and it was breathing."

The crowd roared with laughter.

Michael found it comforting to know that others had to overcome the same fear that was paralyzing him. He was encouraged by the woman's story. She had two children, and the way she figured it, rejection was going to be part of her life no matter what she did. If she made the calls, she would face some rejection on her way to financial independence. If she didn't make the calls, she would face rejection in a very different way, like when she wanted retire, but would have to reject that thought because she didn't have enough money. She explained how she refused to let the fear of rejection keep her family from their dreams.

The woman displayed a truly inspirational attitude, and one that Michael decided to emulate. There was no way that a little phone was going to stop him from providing for his family. He thought of Dylan, who was a baby now but would someday be a young man. How would he be able to tell his boy that he found a way for them to live a better life, but he was afraid to make a call? He was not going to let that happen. Michael sat down in a quiet area of the house with his script, a pen, and a cell phone. He put his names list on the table, and started dialing.

The first two calls didn't go very well. His prospects, both friends who he hadn't seen in a while, started asking questions early in the conversation, and even though he was advised against it, Michael's nervous tendencies once again took over as he tried to answer those questions. As a result, both of them said they were not interested in his "opportunity." Michael knew they made their decision based on very little information. He also knew he was still exercising his jawbone a bit too much. Before making the next call, Michael reflected upon the conversations he had on the yacht. He remembered the importance of maintaining his posture when he invited people over to his house. Posture. That was the missing ingredient which was required if he intended to fill his living room with potential business partners.

He dialed the next number with posture on the forefront of his mind. Michael began the call the way he was taught, by clearing his prospects time with one simple line, "Hey Bob, this is Michael Harper, Do you have a few minutes to talk?"

He found that to be an easy way to start the conversation, but the mistakes he was making earlier came immediately after, when the person said, "Sure, what's up?" At that point, Michael's previous calls consisted of nervous, sometimes incoherent rambling. He would say something like, "I just got involved with a business opportunity that I wanted to tell you about."

If he were on the game show Family Feud, this sentence would give him his first big red "X". When it comes to recruiting for network marketing, one "X" is all you get. Michael had already learned on the yacht that some of the words he was using, like *business opportunity* and *got involved with* were first impression killers.

Instead of continuing to make those mistakes, this time he followed his company's script precisely. After clearing his prospects time, Michael spent a few moments asking how their family was, then he mentioned that he was calling because he had a business idea he wanted to run by them. After providing some information, he invited them to his house. When questions were asked, Michael confidently replied with, "That's a great question. I'm having a few people over tomorrow and Wednesday night to watch a brief presentation that will answer all of your questions. I would like you to attend one of them, but I need to know if you can make it because I have a lot of people who have been expressing an interest in this. So which night is better for you?"

Michael was surprised at how many people committed to come see the details of his company's program. This was partially because he was harnessing the power of curiosity by not providing all the details over the phone. He also had no problem taking the opportunity to look at his business away from people who weren't open-minded. If a person resisted any invitation to check out the details before they made a decision, he would say, "Bob, I can tell this isn't for you. That's no problem. I'll just take you off my list. Thanks for your time."

More than once, that line, or one like it, caused his prospect to make a complete turnaround and express more interest than they had earlier in the conversation. *All because people want what they can't have*, Michael reminded himself.

While making his calls, Michael had a revelation. He realized that he actually learned more about the company's system by making a dozen phone calls than he previously did by listening to CD's and reading starter materials. He concluded that the best way to learn, and overcome fear, is by doing the thing that you fear. Making those phone calls enabled him to get a feel for how conversations play out over the phone, which enabled him to practice navigating his way through a proper invitation.

Over the next two weeks, Michael didn't have a successful meeting. He had nine successful meetings. The first two were at his house, where he filled his living room with curious people. Two more were at the homes of a couple of new teammates he had just signed on. The other five were one-on-ones that Michael scheduled over lunch and at other people's homes after work. Blake was right about the one-on-ones. Michael was able to focus completely on the individual or couples he met with, and learn about them and their dreams, better than he would have in a room full of others.

Any time Michael thought of slowing down, he would imagine Blake looking at him with tightened eyes and stressing the words, "If I'm going to help you, then you need to trust me and do what I tell you." He also thought about how pleased Blake was when he told the millionaire that he listened to all twenty-five of the CD's he was given instead of just ten, like Blake had originally asked. He wanted to show the millionaire that he was willing to do more than what was expected. He owed that much to Blake, and to his wife, Kristen.

It's funny how something a person hates can turn out to be something they like when they make one simple change. For example, driving in bumper-to-bumper traffic, which Michael despised, had quickly turned out to be one of his favorite parts of the day. The reason for this change was simple, personal growth CD's. Instead of listening to the radio, Michael was filling his mind with information that could set his family free. The speakers on the CD's were arming Michael with the thoughts and techniques he needed to improve every area of his life. He was learning how to deal with difficult people and why it is important to give your best effort in everything you do. This information helped him improve his attitude about challenges he encountered in life, which in turn, helped him improve his performance at work. He was even learning how to have balance in life.

The speakers said many things on those audios that influenced Michael. As a true believer of personal growth, Michael didn't rely solely on CD's to help shape his thinking. He also picked up copies of the books that Blake had recommended and began reading Dale Carnegie's *How to Win Friends and Influence People*. By reading this book, instead of the sports page of his local newspaper, he continued to recondition his thinking. Chapter one alone, where Carnegie urged his reader not to criticize, condemn or complain, was worth the price of the book.

Even though his journey had just started, and he struggled with things that were unfamiliar to him, Michael sensed that his life was beginning to change directions for the better. It made him realize how incredible it is that we, as human beings, let the things we fear keep us from moving in the direction of our dreams. Simple things, like making a phone call to share a potentially life-changing business idea with a friend, could paralyze the same person who wouldn't think twice to call that same friend to see if they wanted a free coupon for dinner at a local restaurant.

Because Michael took action and refused to give in to his fear, he had nine good meetings in two weeks, which brought in several new teammates. He was no longer feeling like he was alone in the forest chopping down trees with a dull axe. He now felt as if there were others doing it with him. Momentum started to kick in and he began earning money. There were occasional seeds of doubt and fear, and of course some critics, but Michael was on his way to a better life. He also knew he was going to have to share his progress with Blake, so he kept moving forward, anticipating his next meeting with the millionaire.

Burning Desire

BLAKE AND LAURA Easton lived in a waterfront mansion on the Navesink River in Middletown, New Jersey. That much Michael knew. He also knew, from his first visit to the millionaire's office nearly a month ago, they lived on one of the most beautiful streets in one of the most prestigious neighborhoods in the state. He heard stories from others in the business about how beautiful the Easton's home was, which added to the mystique, and the excitement, he was feeling. In fact, he wasn't sure what excited him more, sharing the results from his meetings, or seeing the waterfront mansion. Yes, Michael was very excited to finally see the millionaire's mansion, and although she wouldn't admit it, Kristen was as well.

Michael pulled up to the front gate. Before he could open his door to press the call button, the gate doors opened. They entered the property and drove straight, down the magnificent winding cobblestone driveway that was lined with antique lampposts, stately sycamore trees and beautifully manicured landscaping. The flowers were vibrant with color and in full bloom. The property sat on a green rolling pasture and was meticulously maintained.

As they approached the mansion, Michael and Kristen caught a glimpse of the water where three jet skis were weaving their way through the wake of a large boat. They drove slowly, passing a stable where horses were being fed. Next to the stable was a small equestrian center where, they would find out later, Laura practiced her mastery of riding. The driveway ended in a circular pattern with a jaw-dropping fountain in the center. It was six feet high with four detailed dolphins carved into the base. The second level was shaped like a large seashell with three fishes protruding from the stone. The top level was a smaller version of the second. Water was flowing from the mouths of all the fish into the basin below. It was dramatic and eye-catching, like something one would expect to see in Paris or Rome. The fountain, although impressive, was overshadowed by the stunning home, which was more than 20,000 square feet of elegance.

"Holy cow!" was all that Michael could say.

The exterior of the three-story mansion was characterized by alternating bands of rough and smooth finished gray stone, and was enlivened by porticos, piazzas and bay windows. There were four walkout balconies on the second floor, each covered by rooftops that were supported with rounded columns.

Michael and Kristen parked in the driveway, gathered the baby from his car seat and walked up to the front door. They were like two giddy kids. It wasn't every day they dined in a mansion with such quality people. Michael was holding Dylan in his left arm. He reached out, pressed the doorbell, and could hear a tune chime from outside. "Sounds like ours," he joked. They both laughed.

Michael was looking forward to introducing Kristen to Blake. He was equally as excited about meeting Blake's wife, Laura and seeing their amazing home. The door opened and the millionaire greeted them with a smile.

"Blake?" Michael was confused.

"You were expecting…?" Blake waited for Michael to finish his sentence.

"A butler."

Blake laughed, "The day I can't do a simple thing like open my own door is the day my ego needs a reality check."

"Blake, this is my wife, Kristen, and our son, Dylan."

"It's a pleasure to meet you, Kristen, please come in." Blake reached out and caressed the baby's cheek with his finger. "Hi Dylan… he's beautiful."

"Thank you," Kristen replied. "*Your home* is beautiful."

The two-story entry foyer featured a breathtaking Cinderella staircase that provided the extravagant entrance that one would have expected. Laura was walking down one side. She also greeted the couple with a smile. After introductions, and true to Blake's comment about his wife's adoration for babies, it didn't take long before Laura was holding Dylan in her arms while giving the couple a tour of their mansion.

It was the true definition of elegance. The home consisted of more than twenty rooms, which included eight bedrooms, two living rooms, a great room, a solarium and an office/library—most of which provided exquisite river views. Each room boasted unique custom decorative moldings, coffered ceilings, fireplaces with brilliantly carved custom mantles, and gleaming hardwood floors. The magnificent great room, which featured a 25-foot ceiling and a gallery of priceless artifacts, was unsurpassed by anything the couple had ever seen. In the back yard was an expansive covered porch with ceiling fans, comfortable outdoor furniture, a full bar and a surround sound audio system that provided a perfect setting to enjoying outdoor entertaining and tranquil sunsets. To the left was an infinity edge pool that looked as if the water flowed directly into the river itself. There were a hundred small, glimmering lights placed on the bottom of the pool that, in the evening, gave the impression that you were looking up at the sky.

Beyond that, there was a tennis court and a small set of bleachers. *They actually have bleachers,* Michael thought. He laughed when he realized that the attached garage was twice the size of the home he and Kristen were living in. Straight out, over the river, was a long pier with a gazebo on the end and a thirty-five foot cabin cruiser that Blake used for entertaining. The home and all its contents were nothing short of fabulous.

After a tour of the mansion, they all settled into the gourmet kitchen for a wonderful dinner that Laura prepared. Blake bragged about his wife's cooking and insisted that she was better than any personal chef they could hire. It was clear to Michael and Kristen that the couple had a strong marriage based on a foundation of unconditional love and respect for each other. As the four dined, they shared stories about the town they all grew up in and had a wonderful conversation on a variety of topics, which included boating, books, horses, travel, shopping, and of course, babies. After dinner, the ladies continued their conversation in the kitchen as Michael and Blake went into the library to talk business.

Blake's home office was as luxurious as the rest of the mansion, with beautiful hardwood floors, crown molding and a striking oversized, richly grained, cherry hardwood desk in the center of the room. The walls on each side were covered by beautifully crafted floor-to-ceiling bookshelves. There were easily one thousand books on display, which is why Blake referred to the room as his library.

Blake took a seat behind the desk but remained casual. Michael sat down on the couch, facing Blake.

"So fill me in," Blake said, straightforwardly.

Michael told the millionaire about his meetings and shared with him how much money he had earned so far. He talked about the 'not so great' experience he had with a few bad calls early on, and shared how he turned them around after he recalled the conversations he had with the leaders on the yacht and began to implement the posture techniques they spoke about. Blake was pleased with Michael's progress. He was especially happy that the new entrepreneur had taken the initiative to schedule one-on-ones and in-home meetings for his new teammates.

"To be honest," Michael said, "I worked a lot harder than I normally would have because I knew you would be asking about my progress."

"Making yourself accountable to others is imperative," Blake said. "Especially if they have a vested interest in your success. My accountability partner was a man who owned a chain of restaurant franchises. We were at similar stages in the business and shared the same vision on where we wanted to end up. He helped me stay on track toward reaching my goals, and I did the same for him."

"Did you talk with him often?" Michael asked.

"Every day, and I still do," Blake replied.

"Still?" Michael questioned. He found it odd that a man as wealthy as Blake would find it necessary to have an accountability partner.

"We speak for five minutes at the beginning of each day and discuss our intentions. It helps us both stay focused and make greater progress in less time because we concentrate solely on results. I find that by vocalizing my intentions to someone, I am less likely to drag my feet and more likely to take action and create momentum. The end product of accountability is that you wind up creating a business by design rather than default."

"How can I find an accountability partner?"

"For you it will be easy. You already met some of your up-line. They have obviously taken notice of you."

"As a matter of fact, I did receive a few calls from people who said they were in my up-line and wanted to introduce themselves. A couple of them offered to do a meeting for me."

"Who came in to help you with your first meeting?" the millionaire asked.

"A man named Steve Mosley," Michael replied, "He's been great."

"I know him," Blake said, "He is a great guy, and very knowledgeable about the industry. Have you thought about making him your accountability partner?"

"Actually, I hadn't thought of it, but I'll ask him."

"Great, but I want you to understand that accountability is not something you ask for. It's something that you develop through performance. For example, I wanted to report good news to the man I was accountable to, and because of that, a relationship took place," Blake explained. "Accountability is based on respect. Don't confuse it with management. The top producers, like Steve, will gravitate to people like you who are performing. In that respect, you can actually force your up-line to want to spend time with you because they see, by your actions, that you are serious.

"At your next meeting, spend more time getting to know them. You will be able to tell what their commitment level is by the level they have reached in the business, the things that come out of their mouth and by the way they treat others. I have counseled many new people in the past about committing to an accountability partner. Be sure to choose a person who has developed a business that produces the results you are striving to produce for yourself, or someone who is committed to the same vision that you have. You're always better off being accountable to someone who can provide reliable counsel when you need it. Direct selling is unique compared to traditional business because the other people in the room truly want you to succeed. When you make money, the entire organization becomes stronger and every member of the team you're working with benefits. You won't find much of that in corporate America, because in corporate America, the reality is the better you are at your job the greater the chance your coworkers have of being fired."

"Wow, I never considered that," Michael admitted. He was taken aback by the common sense in what Blake had just shared.

"That makes everything so…" Michael stopped and stared into space as a disbelieving smile came upon his face.

"Clear," Blake said, finishing the sentence appropriately.

Michael looked at Blake and elevated his eyebrows, "Exactly," He agreed. "Now I understand why everything gets so tense at my work when a promotion opens up."

"Like a bunch of seagulls fighting over a french-fry." Blake compared.

"Great analogy," Michael said.

"Thanks." Blake chuckled.

"Every time I'm around you, I become more enthusiastic," Michael replied. He knew this would be a great opportunity to make mention of his latest challenge. "I wish I could keep that energy level up because I feel like I'm heading in the right direction, but I want it to happen so much quicker. To be honest, it's a little frustrating." He admitted.

"Frustration is part of the journey, Michael. But I have always found it a bit odd that people who spend twenty to thirty years of their life doing things that made them broke, often become frustrated when they don't become rich in twenty or thirty days. Would you like me to teach you how to overcome frustration?" the millionaire asked.

"Absolutely."

"Let me begin with a question. If you woke up tomorrow and had a million dollars deposited into your bank account, how would your day look?"

"Pretty darn good," Michael replied.

"I need more than that. How would you feel? What would you do with that time you would normally spend at your job? The time your boss used to own?" Blake asked.

"I'm not sure. I never thought of what it would feel like to have a million dollars," Michael admitted.

"Think about it now," Blake stated, simply. "If your goal is to become wealthy, this is how you start."

Michael pondered the question. "I guess I would take a vacation. Kristen and I have always wanted to go somewhere in the Caribbean."

"Okay, good. Which island?" Blake asked.

"I don't know. I suppose we haven't really looked into it because it seems unrealistic at this point in our lives."

"Nothing is unrealistic Michael. Two plus two doesn't always have to equal four. It can equal whatever you want it to be, especially for the person with faith and an unswerving work ethic. Think outside the box and tell me what island you'd like to vacation on," Blake insisted.

Michael was embarrassed that he didn't know the names of many islands, he just knew he dreamt of sitting on a beach with sand in between his toes and looking out at a crystal blue sea, free from worry and stress. As he pondered the question, he looked up at an oil painting that was framed and hanging on the wall behind Blake. It featured a few islanders walking along the shore on a beautiful sunny day. There was another couple sitting on the beach, in the forefront of the painting, conversing. In the background, the island curved, showing the twisting edge of the colorful shoreline. Two fishermen were on a small boat just off the coast. The painting gave Michael a calm and inviting feeling.

"That one," he said.

Blake didn't have to look back. He knew what Michael was referencing. "That's Martinique, a good choice."

"Have you been there?" Michael asked.

"Many times," Blake replied. His answer did not surprise Michael, and of course, the millionaire knew more than just the islands name.

"Martinique is an island of French charm, class and culture," Blake replied. "The native Arawaks call it the *Island of Flowers*. It's an appropriate name. We toured the rain forest on our last visit. It was incredible. And the beaches are simply breathtaking. Martinique is actually a French colony and has been since the mid-17th century. Many refer to the island as Paris's westernmost suburb. That picture you're looking at is from a famous painter named Paul Gauguin, titled 'Seashore, Martinique'. It captures part of the essence of the island, but you have to see the black sand beaches and the Mount Pelée with your own eyes and tour the rainforest yourself to fully appreciate its natural beauty. By the way, the food is splendid. The forests on the island are full of pineapple, papaya, avocado and banana trees. You'll never want to eat fruit in the states again."

"It sounds wonderful," Michael said.

"It is," Blake assured before asking his next question. "What about Dylan. Have you ever thought about his education?"

"You mean college?"

"Yes."

"Not really. It seems kind of early to be thinking about things like that."

"It's never too early. It would be terrible if your son had the grades and ambition to attend a school like MIT or Princeton, but you didn't have the means to send him there, don't you agree?"

"Of course," Michael admitted.

"That's why it's important that you raise your expectations and enlarge your vision." Blake continued, "Frustration ultimately comes from lack of focus. When you become focused, you become results oriented. I can tell when one of my teammates or clients is results oriented by the questions they ask. If they come to my managers and ask why they can't sell anything, I know that person lacks focus. I would know that same person is focused if he asked a different question."

"Like?"

"'*What are the people who are having success doing that I am not?*'" Blake answered. "That's the correct question to ask. You have to ask the right questions if you want to get the right answers. In all team-oriented businesses like ours, you don't want to ask why your people aren't doing anything. The proper question would be '*what do I need to do to create momentum?*'"

Michael pulled a small pad out of his back pocket. "May I?" he asked, pointing to a pen on the millionaire's desk.

"Of course," Blake picked up a platinum Mont Blanc pen and handed it to Michael before resuming the conversation, "Most people, and companies for that matter, have fuzzy vision. If you want to succeed, you must have extreme clarity and a clear vision of what you want to accomplish. Focus on the prize, not the price."

Michael stopped writing and looked up at Blake, "When you say price, do you mean the cost?"

"No, I mean the price in terms of sweat equity. '*What*' you need to do is not nearly as important as figuring out '*Why*' you are doing it. You have to focus on the end results and you can't do that if you haven't determined what those results are going to be."

"Set a goal and keep your eye on that goal," Michael said, as he jotted that down, acknowledging that he was beginning to understand Blake's lesson.

"Exactly, the best way to overcome frustration is to clearly define what you are running towards. It has to be something that you love enough to take risks, jump over hurdles and break through the brick walls that are always going to be placed in front of you. If you don't have that kind of feeling for what it is you are doing, you'll stop the minute things get tough. Once you find that thing, keep it in front of you at all times so you never forget what you are playing for." Blake pointed at a photo collage on the wall by the study door.

"What's that?" Michael asked.

"Take a look."

Michael stood, walked over and looked at the collection of pictures, which included a private jet, an island and a black and white photo of what appeared to be *The Majestic Treasure*. "That's your yacht," Michael said.

"Not mine, that's the *Corsair IV*, J.P. Morgan's famous yacht. She was built in the 1930's." Blake explained, "I put that picture on my vision board nearly twenty years ago. Long before I could afford a yacht of my own."

"Vision board?"

Blake stood up and walked toward him. "A vision board is a collage of images, pictures and affirmations of your dreams and desires. Some people call it a dream board." He reached up and removed the picture of the yacht. "The key is to place the board somewhere in your home where you will see it every day. Doing this will remind you of your goals. You can only remove a picture when it comes to fruition."

"Do you believe vision boards work?"

"Did you enjoy your time on my yacht?"

"Good point," Michael said with a smile.

"The *Corsair IV* set transatlantic crossing records and grabbed headlines for the better part of the decade," Blake said, clearly admiring the picture.

"I can feel your passion for yachting when you talk," Michael said.

"Passion comes from romancing your dreams, Michael. Cutting out pictures is just the beginning. You want to step into those pictures."

"How?"

"Go out and test drive your dream car, and walk through open houses in a neighborhood that you'd like to live in.

Visualize yourself owning the things you desire. If you do that long enough and work hard enough, you'll find yourself achieving much more than the average person, who quits when the going gets tough."

"I can't help but to recognize that you seem to have been motivated by both fear and passion," Michael said.

"That's an accurate observation. In my life, inspiration and desperation have both served a purpose. Both have prompted me to take action that has created reward," Blake replied.

The millionaire walked over to his desk, took a 3" x 5" index card out of his top drawer and handed it to Michael.

Michael looked at the card, then turned it over and looked at the other side. Both sides were blank. "What's this?"

"After you define your reasons for building the business, summarize the top five and write them down on that card. Make sure you never leave your house without it in your pocket. Whenever fear and doubt creep into your mind, pull that card out of your pocket and read it. If your dream is big enough, nothing will stop you. There are few obstacles in life that are big enough to stop a person who has a burning desire."

"How do I know if the things I put on my board and on this card are the ones that will provide that burning desire I need to accomplish my dreams?"

"That's a *great* question, Michael." Blake said, emphasizing the word great. The millionaire slowly inhaled and released his breath before answering. "If I placed a twenty foot wooden plank on the ground and offered you one hundred dollars to walk across it, would you do it?"

"Of course."

"What if I went to the top of a thirty story building and placed this same plank as a bridge to the next door building, would you walk across it then?" the millionaire asked.

"Heck no," Michael replied, without hesitation. "I have a fear of heights."

Blake turned and faced Michael head-on, "Close your eyes."

"Excuse me?"

"Go ahead, close your eyes. I want you to visualize something."

Michael complied with the request and closed his eyes. Blake continued, "Whatever you do, don't open your eyes until I tell you, do you understand?"

"Yes." Michael was still unsure where this was going.

"I want you to visualize being on top of that roof. I want you to walk to the edge and look down. Everything below you looks small, right?" Michael was beginning to feel uncomfortable as the millionaire moved closer, "When you look over the edge, you feel yourself getting a little dizzy, so you raise your head. When you do, you see the plank going to the building next door. It's old and slightly warped. Would you walk across it for one hundred dollars?"

"No," Michael answered, quicker than he did before. He could feel his heart beat increasing.

"What if I offered you one thousand dollars?"

"I can't do it. Not for a thousand, not even for ten thousand. I want to, but I can't," Michael said affirmatively.

"Okay, keep your eyes closed. I want you to imagine this situation." Blake said, as he came closer, closing the space between the two so he could speak quietly into Michael's ear. "On the other building are your wife and child... and the building is on fire. The flames are inches away and the roof looks like it's going to collapse. Can you see their faces?" the millionaire asked.

"I don't want to see that," Michael admitted, his body temperature began to rise.

"Do this Michael, trust me... Can you see their faces?" Michael's mind began to visualize the scenario. He could see the terror in his wife's eyes. He could hear Dylan crying. He could feel the sweat accrue on his forehead. He could even feel the radiant heat on his face. His heart began to beat faster.

"Michael, can you see their faces?"

"Yes," drawing a rapid, deep breath, "I can."

"You're the only one who can save them. Will you cross it now?"

"YES!" He answered with an assertiveness he had not shown the millionaire up until that point. "I would do whatever I had to do to save them!" His breathing was rapid. The sweat was now visible.

"Open your eyes," the millionaire directed. Michael did as he was told and the tenseness immediately left his body. He knew this was an exercise, but the emotions he just experienced were so real that the simple act of opening his eyes and not seeing his family in distress enabled his body to relax.

"That..." Blake began, pumping his fist and grinding his teeth as the word exited his mouth, "is burning desire." He peered into Michaels eyes, "When you want something that badly, you'll have it."

As he spoke those words, Blake displayed a fervor that Michael hadn't seen in any person before. It was clear that Blake Easton possessed a definiteness of purpose and a burning desire to possess the things that were important to him. Michael wanted to have that trait. He wanted others to see that same fire in his eyes. He wanted others to recognize that his dream was big enough to overcome any obstacles placed in his path.

Blake took the blank index card out of Michael's hand. "You have to be passionate about this..." the millionaire stressed, as he held the card up and shook it, maintaining that fire in his eyes and fervor in his voice. "Because if you ever lose your will to fight, someone who has a will to fight will control you." Michael felt chills travel up and down his spine, the kind that a person gets when he is overcome with a desire to win. "Brick walls aren't there to keep you out, they're there so you can show how bad you want to get in."

Big Rocks First

KRISTEN AND LAURA HAD more in common than either of them would have expected. For starters, they both loved children, working out, and single cup coffee makers. They were also fans of "the Boss," Bruce Springsteen, who had once lived only a few miles from the Easton's. The two of them had become very comfortable with each other in a very short time. Michael would have been pleased with the way things were going between them, but it was better that he was not in the room. Michael's absence gave the chance for Kristen to open up to Laura about her true feelings about the business.

Laura listened as Kristen poured her heart out about her childhood and how her father was always "somewhere, doing something," when all she wanted was for him to show that he was interested in her life and proud of her. She nearly came to tears when she admitted her fear of that same scenario developing with her and Michael.

"I want the business to work," she stressed, "I just don't want to end up like my parents did. My father, working all the time, made my mother resent him so much that she divorced him. I know he thought he was doing the right thing, but they were on two different pages."

Laura continued to listen intently. She, like her husband, had been in network marketing long enough to hear it all. Kristen's comments did not come as a surprise. "Many couples come into the business with those same fears," she said.

"They do?"

"Yes," Laura said, as she reached over the table and grabbed Kristen's hand to reassure her. "This business is different. You can build a big business together and remain happily married. In fact, you can do it in a way that it will strengthen your marriage."

"How?" Kristen asked.

"By working as a team," Laura explained. "Imagine how strong your marriage would be if you achieved financial stability while working together, each contributing equally."

"But, I'm not like Michael. He's good at talking to people. I'm not."

"You can become good at it. I have spoken with thousands of women throughout the years and I am constantly in awe of how powerful some of them are. Did you know that seventy percent of the people who join network marketing companies are women?"

"No, I didn't."

"It's true, and many of the top income earners in the world are women. In fact, six of the top ten producers in our company are women."

"That's impressive."

"I agree, but what's more impressive is the fact that some of these women started off just like you. They had to learn and grow, just like everybody else, but even if you aren't ready to go out and build the business, that doesn't mean you can't contribute in other ways," Laura added. "The most important thing you can do right now is support Michael."

"I do," Kristen replied. "Deep down inside, he knows that."

"He shouldn't have to look deep down inside. You should tell him as often as possible, so he doesn't have to wonder. Our husbands need to hear us tell them we are proud of what they are doing as much as we need to hear them tell us they love us. Communication is the key," Laura explained. "And that goes both ways."

"I agree," Kristen admitted.

"You also need to define what you want out of this. You already know what Michael wants, but what are *your* goals and dreams? Do they align with his? Do you both put family first? This all needs to be discussed out in the open."

"I do put family first, but I'm not sure if Michael does."

"Why do you say that?"

"We were invited to dinner at my mother's house last weekend and he said he couldn't come because he had already scheduled a meeting," Kristen explained. "So we ended up rescheduling dinner on another day."

"Blake did the same thing our first year in the business."

"Really?"

"Sure. For the first couple of years I almost resented the fact that he was spending so much time helping other people. This was before I started reading books and attending events. Once I started doing that, I began to understand what we had our hands on. I started to reach out to some of my contacts and guess what?"

Kristen was on the edge of her seat, "What?"

"I'm proud to say that I am responsible for two of the largest teams in our organization— including the one that led to you."

"Wow! You mean to tell me that a good portion of your net worth came after you started building the business?"

"Quiet," Laura whispered, while holding her finger in front of her mouth. "Blake doesn't like to admit it."

They both laughed.

"Once we were on the same page," Laura continued, "we'd schedule dinners or occasional parties around our business. Sometimes we even missed a party altogether, but early on, we sat down and determined what we were willing to sacrifice in order to achieve our dreams. We loved informal family events, but we wouldn't cancel an important business meeting just to get together with family members when we could reschedule the family event instead." Laura clarified, "That was our way of putting our family first. If we cancelled the meeting, we would wake up the next day, no closer to our dreams than the day before."

"I hadn't thought of it that way," Kristen confessed.

"My husband would always tell me that cancelling a qualified appointment would violate the law of the rocks," Laura said. She could relate to the blank look on Kristen's face because she probably had that same look when she first heard the term, which needed clarification.

Laura elaborated by saying, "The law of the rocks is the topic of one of Blake's most popular classes. I'll do my best to explain it to you in a way that I understood it. Imagine you have a one-gallon bucket on the table in front of you. Also on the table are four elements. They are water, sand, pebbles and large rocks.

Imagine that each of those elements represented a different activity that you do on a daily basis.

"The *water*, for example, represents chores around the house. That includes everything from grocery shopping to paying bills. The *sand* represents family related responsibilities, such as attending parties and other events. The *pebbles* represent everything you do to earn income. This includes your full-time jobs. The *bigger rocks* represent the actual appointments you set up to show our business plan. Most people begin to fill their buckets up with water, sand, and pebbles. In other words, they are busy, very busy, doing the things they have been conditioned to do their entire adult life. So busy in fact that when it comes time for the rocks, they realize their bucket is already full and there is no room, or more specifically, no time to do the activity that can set their family up for financial success, which is showing the presentation to qualified prospects. This is what the majority of people who say they are too busy to build the business are actually doing. They have the time…"

"They're just busy doing things they could postpone or do another time," Kristen finished. Her body language expressed that she understood and agreed with the point that Laura was making.

"It's not that you shouldn't do those other things," Laura explained. "They are important, but sometimes we need to prioritize and make sacrifices to ensure that we get what we want out of life. Otherwise…" Laura glanced over at Dylan, who was taking a nap on the couch nearby, "there's a chance that Dylan may grow up wanting things you and Michael may never be able to provide. Several years ago, Blake and I made the decision that we would do the things we need to do today, so we can do the things we want to do tomorrow. Tomorrow is here, and we don't regret one decision we have made. Your son, who may travel the world with you the way Blake and I have, will never ask you why you celebrated his birthday on Sunday instead of Saturday one weekend when he was too young to even know what a birthday is."

Kristen got it. She knew firsthand how much she and Michael were struggling with finances. If they were going to change their reality, they would have to both be willing to make a few sacrifices and prioritize.

"You have a bigger role in all of this than you think," Laura said. "If you are not behind your husband or standing by his side, he will feel like the world is against him and he will not make it."

"What you are saying sounds nice, but I am so afraid of growing apart."

"Then don't," Laura said, in the most plainspoken, straightforward way possible. "Talk with Michael and establish your house rules like Blake and I did."

"What were they?"

"He never walked into the house after working while on the cell phone, and he spent time with me before he picked up the phone and started doing the business. When he did get to business, he set specific time limits. If he told me he was going to work for two hours, after the two hours were up, he would shut his computer and turn off his cell phone and spend time with me. If you decide to work the business equally, one can cook while the other is working, then you can sit down for dinner. After dinner, you can reverse roles when it comes to doing dishes and cleaning up. Take turns putting your son to bed, and never let him see you argue about the business, or anything for that matter, be an example so when he grows up, he looks for a spouse that will support him and work alongside of him the way you and Michael will. Do you think you can do those things?"

"Yes," Kristen answered.

"I know you can too," Laura agreed. "Another thing you should do is listen to the CD's and read the books that Michael does. If you do this, you will both be in sync with the business and growing at a similar pace. I have seen couples that struggled because one was constantly improving, while the other was remaining status quo. They eventually become slightly disconnected."

"I do have to admit, ever since Michael has met your husband, his outlook on life has improved so much. I figured the CD's had something to do with it."

"They absolutely do," Laura said.

Kristen took a deep breath. "I'm not sure how yet, but I'm going to get more involved. I know it's the right thing to do."

"It is. I promise," Laura said. "There's one more thing I want you to do along the way."

"What's that?" Kristen asked.

"Reward yourself," Laura replied. "Set goals together, and reward yourself when you reach them. When you hit a level in the business that you worked hard for, get a babysitter for the night and go out to dinner together, and maybe a movie. As the accomplishments get more significant, the rewards should match."

"I'd like that," Kristen admitted.

"I thought you would." Laura smiled. "That's been my favorite part of the journey."

The new friends continued their conversation, talking about everything one could imagine talking about.

Pension Prisoner

A CANDLE BURNED on a small table in the corner of the mentor's library and filled the room with the scent of honeysuckle. Ironically, it was one of Michael's favorite scents because it caused him to recall one of his fondest early memories of his father. Growing up, the Harpers had a large honeysuckle bush on their front lawn. When the bus dropped the kids off on the corner of his block, Michael's father would be there to greet them on his days off. Even though Michael's mother repeatedly asked him to stop, his father enjoyed picking flowers off the bush with the kids and showing them how to suck the flavor out. From his father's point of view, it helped him manage the ever-growing shrub, which he often complained was a hassle to maintain.

As Michael's mind wandered, the mentor was contemplating the best way to answer his question about how he could improve his closing ratio. The mentor believed that people learn more from a story.

"My wife and I own a set of expensive knives," Blake started. "As a matter of fact, they're the most exclusive eating knives that I know of. To this day, I'm not sure how, or even why we bought them. What I do know is that the salesman assumed the close. He did this so well, in fact, that we ended up purchasing these knives that we didn't want or need. I also know that the scissors that came with these knives will cut through a nickel."

Michael laughed.

"Really, he proved it right in front of me, with my nickel," Blake added, before laughing along with him. "I remember looking right at him, sitting there in his suit, talking about how great these knives are and all I kept thinking was, I don't care what he's selling, I'm not buying."

"How did he turn you into a sale?" Michael asked.

"He had so much belief in his product that he had the edge. After he demonstrated how great these knives were, the only logical question for him to ask was, 'Which set would you like to eat with tonight?' As he asked this question, he placed the applications down in front of us, and with pen in his hand he asked the second question."

"Which was?" Michael asked.

"Would you like to pay for them in full or would you prefer our easy payment plan?" Blake replied.

"And that was it?" Michael said with a puzzled look.

"That was it," Blake said. "I personally do not believe that this salesman made a sale after every presentation he did, but I do know that he *dramatically* increased his chances of closing the sale by the assumptions he chose to believe in. That man gave me one of the greatest lessons I had ever learned in sales. Today he's a millionaire."

"What?" Michael was shocked, "From selling knives?"

"No. I was so impressed with him that I shared our compensation plan with him. He tore this thing up."

"That's great."

"You know what else was great?" Blake asked. After a long pause, he answered, "Those knives! We still eat with them today." Michael smiled as Blake summarized his lesson, "The assumptions you make will determine your closing ratio."

"I suppose that's true in any sales organization," Michael said.

"That's correct. In any sales team, the greatest leaders are the best closers, especially in our industry, where the goal is to develop a large team of people. Closing the sale may be the single biggest skill you ever develop to get people to follow you and look at you as a leader. Many times, others will rely on your ability long before they develop confidence in themselves. If you can learn to close the sale, you will instill confidence, and provide your team members with enough belief to keep them going until they develop their own ability to close and lead others."

Michael understood exactly what Blake was talking about. Being new to the industry, he relied on Blake and his up-line to help him sign up new members. His problem was that he often became emotionally tied to the decisions that his prospect made.

If they signed up, he was excited, if they said no, he was upset. Michael recognized this as a shortcoming and knew he would have to stop enabling others to affect his emotions.

"Are there any techniques you use to assume the close?" he asked.

"The best method I used was to identify the most common objections that we usually hear and address them throughout my presentation beforehand. Think about the most effective presenters you have watched. I am sure those people have a knack for addressing objections within their presentation. People think these presenters are extremely talented, and some are, but a successful presenter moves people to action. He has mastered the art of being relatable through either personal stories, or third party testimonies. Both methods offer simple solutions to common objections such as not enough time or lack of money."

Blake could tell Michael was struggling with something. "What else is on your mind?" he asked.

"A couple days ago I ran into a guy I went to high school with. We were having a conversation and I brought up my business. I asked if he wanted to take a look at it. He laughed at me and said he wouldn't waste his time. He said he's been there, done that and everyone thinks they're going to get rich in direct selling but no one ever does."

"Interesting," Blake replied, "What does your friend do for a living?"

"He has a pretty good job. He works for the Post Office."

"Ahhh, a pension prisoner," Blake said as he walked over and leaned on the windowsill.

"Pension prisoner?"

"There's a large segment of society that believes their pension is the answer to everything, but all it really does is keep them comfortable enough to prevent them from going out there and taking chances that could produce great financial rewards. He may think that no one gets rich in network marketing, but what do you think his chances are of becoming wealthy while working for the Post Office?"

"Zero," Michael said.

"He is also at the mercy of the economy. By the time he retires, he may not even have a pension. You have to be careful who you take your advice from."

"I've been learning that," Michael said.

"Why would you care what he thinks anyway? He isn't going to pay your mortgage. If you let anyone's comments stop you from accomplishing your dreams, you might as well just put a picture of him on your vision board and look at that every day as a reminder of why you didn't achieve your dreams."

"You have a great perspective."

"You can thank my wife for that," Blake replied.

"You give her a lot of credit. It's refreshing to hear," Michael said.

Blake subtly and repeatedly nodded his head, "She's everything to me. If it wasn't for her, I'd be shining shoes today," He smiled as he recalled a recent experience. "One day we stopped at a gas station and I stepped out to grab a cup of coffee. When I came back to the car Laura was talking with the attendant. They obviously knew each other. As we drove off, I asked who he was and she told me he was her first love. I have to admit, I was jealous at first, then I said to her, *'See, if you married him, you'd be the wife of a gas station attendant today.'* I was proud of myself until she replied, *'No Blake. If I married him, he'd be a multi-millionaire today.'* I believe she was right. I'm very lucky she chose to spend her life with me."

"Do you think luck plays a part in financial success?"

"Maybe a little, why do you ask?"

Michael became serious, "My friend, Dean was one of the three guys who originally went to look at the business presentation with me. After I met with you in your office, I called him back and told him I was going to try it. He said the people who make it to the top in network marketing were lucky."

"Anyone can get lucky if they work hard enough," Blake explained. "What's Dean's story?"

"Well, he actually does have lady luck on his side. His father is the Vice President of a bank. Last I heard, Dean was going to be promoted to Junior VP. I'd definitely say that having his father help push him up the ladder qualifies as luck."

"Do I sense some jealousy?" Blake asked.

Michael shrugged his shoulders. The corner of his mouth curled up. It was his subtle way of saying yes.

"William Penn said, 'The jealous are troublesome to others, but a torment to themselves.' Don't poison yourself with jealousy Michael, there's no room for it," Blake said.

"I know. It's a bad habit," Michael said. "When Dean's parents moved to Middletown, I thought he was going to finally see how difficult it was to get ahead on his own, but I found out that his father helped him with a down payment for a house."

"His parents live in Middletown?"

"Church Road. Not far from here."

"I know where it is—Michael, luck and success don't often share the same sentence." Blake paused for a moment before adding, "As I spend more time with you, it is becoming apparent to me that you spend a lot of time thinking about and sometimes worrying about what other people are saying and doing. Would you agree with that?"

"I suppose so," Michael said. "I sometimes find it hard to ignore what others are saying. I suppose you could say I don't handle criticism very well."

"What do you see when you walk through a cemetery?"

Michael was caught off-guard. He thought about the question and replied, "Um, tombstones."

"I see the end of dreams," Blake replied, with a straight face. "Beneath most of those tombstones are people who died with their dreams still in them. I see books that were never written, songs that were never sung and businesses that were never developed. I see dreams that were never fulfilled, and ninety-nine percent of the time it was because those poor people let others take that dream away from them." Blake pointed at Michael and narrowed his eyes. "Don't you dare let that happen to you! We only have so much time on this earth and you don't want to live with your talents untapped. History books celebrate people who overcome great challenges, they do not celebrate critics."

Michael acknowledged with a nod. Blake looked at his watch. It was nine o'clock. "Do you have time to take a quick drive with me?"

"Sure, where are we going?"

"For a ride," Blake answered, "Let's tell the girls we'll be back in a half hour."

The Compound Effect

LAURA AND KRISTEN had no problem letting the guys go for a drive in one of Blake's toys. It gave them more time to enjoy each other's company. Blake led Michael through the kitchen, down the hall past the maid's quarters and into what the mentor called his "toy barn." When Michael entered the garage, he was speechless. *Seven, eight, nine, ten...* he counted the cars that Blake owned. The mentor's garage looked like a high-end showroom, except these vehicles were a collection of both modern sports cars and vintage beauties.

Among those that captured Michael's eyes were a vibrant red 1956 Ferrari 860 Monza, a blue and white 1966 Ford GT 40 MKII with the number 25 on the side, and a sleek and sophisticated 1925 Rolls Royce Phantom. All of the cars were gorgeous and in pristine condition, but the one that really seized a hold of his imagination was a flawless blue sapphire Aston Martin V12 Vanquish. The car was familiar to Michael. It was Aston Martin's flagship vehicle whose rise to recognition by the wider public came after it was featured as the official James Bond car in the film *Die Another Day.* Just being up close to it, caused Michael's heartbeat to increase. Blake was about to ask him which one he wanted to take a ride in, but Michael's reaction left no doubt in the mentor's mind. He opened a cabinet and reached for the keys.

"Get in," Blake said.

"Are you serious?"

Before Michael could answer, the garage door opened and Blake was behind the steering wheel. He jumped into the passenger seat. They were on the highway in no time. Michael was grinning from ear to ear with the window down and his head back. *Now, this is living,* he thought. It wasn't until Blake took the Middletown exit that Michael realized what was happening.

"You're not going to…"

"Don't worry. I just want you to see something. What's the house address?"

Michael knew the address but he was reluctant to give it, "I think it's 122—but you're not really going to…"

"Michael," Blake looked over at his anxious passenger and stressed, "Don't worry. I just want to show you something."

Michael's smile turned into a slight scowl. He couldn't imagine what the mentor's intentions were. When they arrived at 122, Blake parked across the street. Michael slid down in his seat slightly, but not enough for Blake to address it.

"Is this it?"

"Yes, this is where Dean's parents live."

Blake looked at the home. It was a nice split-level with black shutters and a paved driveway on the right side. The home was not small, but not big either. It was a comfortable size. It resembled the house on both sides of it, only the front of this particular house had little appeal and was in need of some landscaping. That was obvious, even though it was 9:20 pm and dark. They sat there for a moment, looking at the home. All of the lights to the house were off except for the flickering glow of a television coming from behind the drapes of the front window.

Before Blake could explain why he was there, a car came down the street, slowing as it approached the house, and pulled into the driveway. Ironically, it was Dean's father. The man parked his car and turned off the lights. It took about a minute before he slowly exited the vehicle in a wrinkled suit. The man, who was carrying a briefcase, looked worn out, tired, as he walked toward the side door with his head down and shoulders slightly slouched. He fumbled through his keys, trying to locate the one that would open the door then he entered the house through the kitchen, turned on the light and closed the door behind him.

Through the kitchen window, Blake and Michael could see there was no loving greeting. No warm meal waiting for him. The man's wife didn't even come into the room. He opened the refrigerator door, took out a beverage and a cold slice of pizza and sat down at the kitchen table, alone. Then he opened up his briefcase and began to look over some papers. Michael was silent.

"Is this the life you want?" Blake asked. There was a long pause. "Is it?"

"No," Michael said with a whisper.

"This is the life your friend Dean is heading toward. Things aren't always what they appear to be. Sure, he has a nice car and home, but this man is tired and broke, Michael, just at a higher level than most. I'm sure he is a good man, but he works from paycheck to paycheck just like most Americans and he probably sees no end in sight. You see a title, 'VP.' I see a depressed man who's barely getting by." Blake looked at Michael and waited for him to return the gesture. "Michael, have you ever heard of the compound effect?"

Michael shook his head. "No, what is it?"

"Where we are today is an accumulation of the things we do over a long period of time," Blake explained, "The choices this man has made and the habits he has created led him here. Look at that man."

Michael did what Blake asked. Both of them silently observed what appeared to be a sad, tired man.

Softly, Blake asked, "I'll ask you again, do you want that life?"

"No," Michael said.

"Neither does he," Blake stated. "His daily actions have led him to a place where he is just getting by in life. Do you want to get by or get rich?"

"I think you know that answer."

"Then don't ever fall into the trap of working harder instead of smarter, and don't waste your time on jealousy. God has equipped you with everything you need to fulfill your destiny."

Michael's expression made it clear that he understood. Blake opened his door and began to step out. "What are you doing?" Michael asked, hiding his face so he would not be seen when the interior lights illuminated him.

Blake turned to face him, "Would you like to drive?"

"Absolutely," Michael answered. He quickly exited the car and traded places with Blake. He was ecstatic.

On the ride home, Michael learned what Blake meant when he talked about romancing the dream. Driving behind the wheel of what had just become his dream car made him feel empowered and successful. He was a little disappointed when they reached Blake's home because he wasn't ready for the ride to end. Michael drove down the driveway and into the garage.

Before they exited the car, Blake reached over and grabbed Michael's arm to get his attention, then said, "Your friend Dean may not have your best interest in mind. Be careful whom you associate with, your friends should lift you up, not keep you down. They should encourage you, not discourage you. If you intend to succeed, don't take advice from those who haven't accomplished what you are striving for. Did you know that your lifestyle and income will be an average of the five people you spend the most of your time with?"

"No, I didn't."

"There are more than 270,000 millionaires living in Los Angeles County. There are less than fifty in the county you and I were born in. Which county do you think would provide you with a better chance at becoming a millionaire?" Blake asked.

"Los Angeles," he answered. Blake stared at him, but didn't reply. Michael wasn't sure what to say, so he went for the joke, "That's my final answer."

Blake smiled. "Good one," he said, "but your answer is not entirely correct." A confused expression consumed Michael's face, the mentor continued in a serious manner, "The answer to that question is dependent on another more important question, which is, who are you taking counsel from?" Blake explained. "You see, if you live in a county with only one self-made millionaire and you go to that person for financial advice, you'd be better off than a person who lives in Los Angeles County but is taking advice from the five percent of the residents who are broke. LA County may provide opportunity, but opportunity is everywhere for the person who is seeking it. Let the masses go in one direction and convince each other that only the lucky succeed, just make sure you follow those who have accomplished what you are trying to accomplish and you will substantially multiply your own chances of succeeding. Take that into consideration the next time you choose who you are going to spend your time with."

Blake pointed at one of the walls in his garage. Michael followed with his eyes and noticed a sign. It was about five feet long and two feet high. The words written on it were perfect to sum up the conversation.

Michael read them out loud, "People who say it cannot be done should never interrupt people who are doing it." He contemplated the message.

"Don't let yourself be sidetracked by criticism. God rarely uses a person whose main concern is what others are thinking," Blake added.

"Why do people feel the need to criticize others?" Michael asked.

"Because it's easy, I suppose—but criticism is just as easy to overcome," the mentor said.

He loosened and removed his Rolex watch from his wrist and held it up for display.

"If I offered you this watch as a gift and you took it that would be your personal choice." Blake handed the watch to Michael, before continuing, "If I offered you that watch and you refused to take it that would also be your personal choice—the same goes for criticism. If someone says hurtful things, you don't have to accept them. Eleanor Roosevelt said, 'No one can make you feel inferior without your consent.' I feel sorry for the man or woman whose future depends on the opinions and permissions of others. Show me a person who had spent his life avoiding all forms of criticism and I will show you a person who did nothing, said nothing and achieved nothing."

Michael received the message, but the Rolex intrigued him. It was a Cosmograph Daytona, more commonly known as the driver's watch, a truly magnificent piece of art. He placed it on his wrist to see what it would feel like. It was heavier than expected. Michael was surprised to see that he and Blake had a similar sized wrist. "Can I keep the watch?" he asked.

"Not a chance," Blake replied, as he reached out his hand, palm up.

They laughed.

After reuniting with their wives, they sat around the table and shared stories, as well as a few more laughs. Michael and Kristen thanked Blake and Laura for their hospitality and left for home. On their way home, they shared their experiences with each other. It wasn't until they were almost home that Michael realized they had been holding hands the entire time.

19

Carrying Buckets

AFTER SPENDING AN evening at the Easton's estate, it was almost midnight when Michael and Kristen returned home. Michael carried Dylan into his room and gently placed him in his crib. The couple was so enthusiastic from the time they spent with Blake and Laura that they immediately went to work creating their vision board. Michael logged onto his computer to surf the Internet for a picture of the Aston Martin that he had just driven. When he found one, he printed it out and placed it on the board. He did the same with a picture of a Rolex watch and an aerial view of the Island of Martinique.

Kristen found pictures that represented her dreams and placed them on the board alongside Michael's. They were excited and hopeful. Two things they had not been for quite some time. Kristen sat on the floor, looking at the pictures on the board. Michael sat nearby, and watched his wife.

"We have room for one more picture," Kristen said. "What else do you want?"

Michael was silent. Kristen watched curiously as he reached into his pocket and slowly pulled out a crumbled picture, never taking his eyes off his beautiful wife.

"What are you doing?" she asked.

He straightened the photo as good as he could and placed it on the board. It was the photo of the Coach bag Kristen wanted. Her eyes welled. "Where did you get that picture?"

"From the trashcan," he answered.

"You saved it?" she asked.

"I knew you wanted it, I couldn't let you throw away a dream."

Kristen jumped at Michael and hugged him the same way she did on the night he proposed. It was a feeling both of them had forgotten, and one they hoped never to forget again.

They each defined what they want to achieve from the business and determined what they were willing to sacrifice in order to get it. They also defined what roles each of them would take. Michael's primary role would be to contact people, show the business and develop their team. Kristen would also contact people, but her main focus was on developing relationships with their new teammates. They went to bed that evening inspired and in agreement. They had a dream and a plan to achieve it.

The results they achieved throughout the next few months were a reflection of their inspiration. The couple decided to take Blake's advice and do exactly what he and their up-line leaders suggested. They attended weekly meetings and brought guests with them every time. Focus and determination played a huge role in helping them achieve some of the respectable levels of recognition within the company. At the events, the couple was recognized for their achievements.

Michael and Kristen Harper were beginning to make themselves known, but they had a long way to go and much to learn before they would reach their more significant goals. Doubt, fear and frustration continued to be hurdles for Michael, but he consistently educated himself through books and reflecting on the lessons he learned from the mentor.

After reading the first two books that Blake suggested, he moved on to other books that were designed for entrepreneurs and network marketers. These books helped him expand his vision and belief. He still had occasional no- shows and critics, but he began every day by pulling out his 3" x 5" card and reviewing his top five goals to remind himself what he was striving for. It wasn't the material things that motivated Michael. It was the idea of providing the best possible life that he could for his family. It was the goal of making enough money so that they would never have to worry about money.

One evening, he was relaxing after making a few phone calls when he began to think back to the first time he walked into Blake's office. He recalled the paper that the mentor had posted on his wall with the words "mission statement" written on top. He had heard the term, but he was curious what it was. It was too late to call Blake and ask what was on the paper, so he sat down in front of his computer and began researching the term. He learned that a mission statement is a formal, short, written statement of the purpose of an organization. When written correctly, the document is helpful in guiding the actions of that organization. It will also help describe the overall goal, provide a sense of direction, and guide the decision-making process to ensure every action results in progress. Simply put, the mission statement is a powerful summary that will help keep individuals focused and drive an organization forward.

Michael wasn't sure if his new growing team would be ready to develop an organizational mission statement, but he certainly was. He took out a piece of paper and began jotting down notes to help him clarify one simple statement that would define the essence or purpose of the organization he expected to develop and the person he intended to become. He wrote down things like, over-deliver, enrich lives, help others achieve their goals and dreams, and develop long-term relationships.

An hour passed when he looked down at his paper and something occurred to him. His mission statement, although in its infant stages, was mainly about one thing... helping others. *It's a shame so many people misunderstand this industry*, he thought. Michael was clearly thinking about his three friends, Dean, Billy and Tom, who tried to discourage him from getting involved early on.

Michael and Kristen remained focused and determined, but even the most dedicated people tire and contemplate slowing down, especially when they want something to happen "yesterday." When these types of thoughts arose, Michael would lie on the couch next to his sleeping son and gently place the palm of his hand on Dylan's chest to feel his little body expand and contract with each breath. Sometimes he would lean in close enough to hear and feel the air moving in and out of his lungs. He cherished those moments. That was all he needed to pick up the phone, make another call and keep moving forward, telling himself, "Every lap I run, is one less lap he is going to have to in his life." Family came first for Michael. That was his reason for building the business.

The couples' efforts resulted in duplication that started to produce results that could be summed up in two beautiful words... residual income. Those words had become part of Michael's daily conversations with prospects. His favorite way to describe the residual income came from a story in a book he recently read entitled, *The Cash Flow Quadrant*. In the book, author Robert Kiyosaki talked about how he became financially free by building a pipeline to wealth.

Michael loved that book. He appreciated how Kiyosaki explained that every person, depending on where their main source of income came from, can be placed in one of four quadrants. The left side of the quadrant is for employees and self-employed individuals whose income comes in the form of a paycheck. The right side is for individuals who receive their cash from their own businesses or investments.

The story Michael really liked was the one about the village that needed water. Kiyosaki explained that the quaint little village was a great place to visit and live, except for the fact that it only had water when it rained. To solve their problem, the village elders decided to offer a contract to anyone who could supply water to the village daily. The two individuals who volunteered were both awarded temporary contracts, but they both came from different sides of the quadrant.

The first man had employee thinking. So he ran out, bought two steel buckets and began to run from the village to a lake, which was one mile away. Once there, he would fill the buckets, then return and dump them in a well. He repeated that process— day in and day out, exhausting himself, but earning a weekly paycheck.

The second man operated from a different place, the right side of the quadrant. He has wealth mentality. Once awarded the contract, this man disappeared for a while. Instead of purchasing buckets, he developed a business plan, created a corporation, found investors, employed a president to oversee the work, and returned many months later with a construction crew. Over the next twelve months, his crew developed a stainless steel pipeline, which connected the village to the lake. When the pipeline was complete, he announced he could supply cleaner water 24 hours a day, seven days a week, and charge less money in the process.

To compete, the first man went and purchased four more buckets and hired his two sons to give him a hand on nights and weekends. He even promised his boys that the business would belong to them one day. The second man franchised his business in villages throughout the world, developing healthy residual income streams. One of these men lived happily ever after. The other lived a life of financial hardship.

After reading this story, Michael realized he was carrying buckets every day he put on his uniform and went to work at the warehouse. Thankfully, as he began developing his network marketing business, he began to see the rewards of developing a pipeline. His team had grown to the point where he was benefiting from the efforts of others the way only a successful business owner would.

Residual income was the answer to his financial prayers, and duplication was the way they were going to achieve it. As their team continued to expand, Michael and Kristen began to understand a saying they had heard at one of their local events, which was, *Teamwork makes the dream work.*

They continued to reward themselves along the way. Each time a goal was reached, they took the time to do simple things like take a trip to the local ice cream parlor, or see an occasional movie. After months of consistent effort, they reached their first prestigious level in the business, which called for something more than a chocolate almond sundae, which was Kristen's favorite.

Achieving this new level enabled the couple to do something they always wanted to do but could never afford, see *Phantom of the Opera* on Broadway. When Michael and Kristen were married, they wanted to break away from tradition and do a few things differently than most. One of the things Kristen decided to do was walk the aisle to a less traditional song. She chose the song, *All I Ask of You* from Phantom. Up until today, she and Michael had only heard recorded versions of the song. It was invigorating the night they found themselves sitting in the famed Majestic Theater listening to the live version of this beautiful song while they watched the Broadway show. They were even more excited to be sharing the experience with two other couples on their team.

The Broadway show was great, but the fact that they were able to reestablish a savings account for themselves and start a new one for their son provided enough inspiration and satisfaction to help them stay focused.

They were doing well with the business, but Michael was aware of the fact that they had a very long way to go. He continued to counsel with Blake over the phone on a daily basis and taking the millionaire's advice, the couple made the decision to attend a convention his company was holding in Orlando. Michael didn't know what to expect, but he knew all the leaders in his company would be there. If they were all there, then he and Kristen needed to be there as well. They registered for the event, and encouraged their serious team members to do the same.

Five months had passed since they had dinner at Blake and Laura's house. It was late in November when the couple received an invitation in their mailbox. Michael opened the envelope and read it to Kristen. *"Blake and Laura Easton cordially invite you to attend their annual gathering at The Avenue Restaurant in Pier Village as they celebrate this holiday season."* They quickly and enthusiastically arranged to attend the event.

Move the Marbles

MICHAEL AND KRISTEN wanted to dine at The Avenue Restaurant since it opened three years ago. Recently, the restaurant was recognized in *New Jersey Monthly Magazine* as one of the state's top dining experiences. It was celebrated as much for its well-appointed atmosphere, as for its splendid cuisine. The Avenue could best be described as a cross between the Parisian brasserie and the luxurious beaches of St. Tropez, on the Atlantic beachfront.

The restaurant, which was located in the Pier Village section of Long Branch, brought elegance and sophistication to Jersey Shore dining with its dramatic ceilings, sleek floor-to-ceiling windows, spectacular ocean view, and pearl colored marble tiles that shimmered when the lights from above reflected on them. Pier Village featured extravagant oceanfront residences and more than thirty boutiques and restaurants. Overall, the village could be described as elegance by the sea, and The Avenue Restaurant was its main feature.

The holiday party gave the couple good reason to dress up. Michael wore slacks and a sports coat while Kristen wore a charming cocktail dress. Although The Avenue offered valet service, the couple decided to park at the opposite end of the village. It was warm for December, a beautiful night for a walk and there was no better place to enjoy one. They strolled along the boardwalk hand in hand, passing various storefronts and an acoustic guitar duo that was performing Beatles hits for a moderate size crowd.

At the center of the village was an oversized gazebo where a few couples had paused to embrace the atmosphere. Michael and

Kristen decided to take a few minutes and do the same. They leaned on the railing and looked out at a few of the kids who were playing on the beach. One of which had a small bag of French fries and was tossing them into the air, one at a time, as a group of flying seagulls fought over them.

"What are the odds?" Michael chuckled as he recalled the conversation about corporate America that he had with Blake on the yacht.

"What?" Kristen asked.

"It's nothing. I was just thinking about something Blake said to me," he answered.

The ocean waves were swelling up and crashing on the shore. These weren't ideal surfing conditions, but Michael couldn't help but to notice two surfers in full-body wetsuits sitting on their boards looking out at the ocean. It was as if they were there more for tranquility than for sport.

"Did you happen to bring our camera?" Michael asked.

"I did. Do you want it?"

"Yes," Michael replied.

He took a quick photo to capture the moment before they continued walking the boardwalk.

When they entered the restaurant, the maître de asked their names and scanned the list. "Welcome to The Avenue," he said, inviting the couple in.

The Avenue was everything they expected and more. To the right was a twenty-five foot bar that resembled the hull of a ship. In the center of the five-thousand square-foot space was an oversized double-sided fireplace, emanating a warm glow with comfortable lounge chairs on each side for patrons to socialize before and after their meals. Although the sun was setting, outdoor floodlights over the seating deck were facing the ocean and illuminating the surf and sand.

The restaurant was full with people dressed in professional but casual attire, all of whom were there to celebrate the holidays with the Easton's. Michael wondered if they were all members of Blake's organization. Initially, the couple didn't find their hosts in the crowd so they began to mingle with others. Being dressed up in a room with ambitious people made Michael feel more successful. Just a few months ago, he was dining at a franchise chain in middle of a mall. Tonight he was at the most exclusive party in the state.

The conversations they had were not like those they had become accustomed to in their usual circle. There were no complaints about quarterbacks, the weather, or the price of gas. Everyone seemed happy and the topics of discussion ranged from a variety of interesting subjects, each beginning with a friendly introduction. Michael recognized some of the people he met from events he attended or from his companies top achiever newsletter, but to his surprise, many of the guests were not in the business. Some were friends or family members of the Easton's and a few were business associates and partners from some of Blake's other business ventures. They were respectful professionals and high- quality people. Michael vowed to pursue the same caliber of people as partners for his networking team.

Kristen was the first to notice Blake and Laura. They were sitting in a corner, conversing with others. The couple walked over to say hello. Blake stood up to greet them, raising his voice slightly so he could be heard over the crowd and music he said, "Michael, Kristen, I'm so glad you made it."

The four of them picked up their conversation as if no time had passed since the last time they were all together at the Easton's house.

A waitress carrying a tray of hors-d'oeuvres walked over. The aroma coming from the tray caught the mentor's attention, "You have to try one of these," Blake said, reaching for a delightful variation of the standard bacon-wrapped scallop.

Michael followed Blake's lead and was not disappointed, "Wow, that's terrific."

"And how is Dylan?" Laura asked.

"Getting bigger, he's walking now. We're just trying to keep up with him." Kristen said with a smile.

"I told you time goes by fast," Laura said.

"You're so right," Michael conceded, before scanning the crowd and commented on how polite everyone at the party was.

"This is a great group of people to associate with," the mentor agreed. "So, talk to me. How is your team developing?"

It had been six months since Michael had signed his application. The results they had achieved so far were enough for them to taste success, but not enough for either of them to consider leaving their jobs. Michael felt great about the fact that he had solved the problems that he had encountered earlier in the business. He had overcome his fear of the phone and he had learned how to carry himself with true posture. As a result, many of his team members had begun looking to him for advice. He was an example of what could happen when you put a modest amount of effort into your business for a short period of time, there was only one problem—no one on his team was putting forth the effort he did. The way he expressed this to Blake was by simply stating the obvious, "No one on my team is doing what it takes to build a business."

Michael thought he was in a unique situation, but in reality, if Blake had a dollar for every time he heard someone complain about their groups' lackluster performance, he would have doubled his net worth. Blake knew that Michael had passed the first test. Most people would quit or make excuses why they couldn't build a business, but Michael pushed through his fears and continued to keep his eyes on his goals. Blake was proud of him for that. He also knew that Michael was now dealing with a new set of problems.

"I really want this," Michael stressed, "I've been helping my team every chance I get, but I can't seem to get anyone else to do anything, and I don't know why."

Blake took Michael by the shoulder and quickly led him to a quiet corner of the room. Once there, the mentor bluntly asked, "How many personal presentations have you done in the last thirty days?"

It took Michael a few moments to ponder the question, before stating, "I've been doing a lot of meetings for my teammates."

"That's fine Michael, working in depth is important, but my question is how many *personal* presentations have you done?"

The question made Michael squirm. No one could deny that he had been working hard building his business, but Blake had previously spoken with him about the difference between working hard and working smart. He contemplated a few quick options on how he could best answer the question. In the end, the truth had to come out, "None."

"Therein lies your problem. You need to get back to moving the marbles."

"Excuse me?"

"The only way to guarantee success is by moving marbles." Blake replied. "Let me put it this way, every top producer became a producer first, which you are, but before you can be recognized as someone at the top of your game, you, like everyone else who succeeds in network marketing, will have to conduct a certain amount of presentations. Would you like to know how many?"

"Yes."

"So would I. But there is no set number. The truth is, that number is different for everyone, but I promise you, it's not that drastically different. The bottom line is that you have an exact number of qualified presentations it will take for you to make it to the top, just as I did. Your number may be 127, 205, or 351, but it is definitely there," Blake said.

"But, what does this have to do with marbles?" Michael asked.

"Here's what I want you to do. As soon as you can, go purchase two glass jars, at least two quarts in size. Then purchase 200 marbles. Place all 200 marbles in a jar labeled prospects, and then label the empty jar, presentations. The goal is simple. Move the 200 marbles from one jar to the other. Right now, you are managing your team. You may have moved forty marbles into your freedom jar, but your number is 240. Right now you are messing with that jar that has forty marbles in it when you should really be out there..."

"Moving more marbles," Michael replied.

"That's right, and the best part is you choose how fast you want to move them from one jar to the next. You can move 4-5 per month for 3 ½ years, or you can move 20 per month for 10 months. The speed is up to you. Whatever you do, don't try to beat the odds. Many salespeople begin this process, and somewhere about marble number 25 they know just enough to be dangerous. That's just about the time when they have made just enough sales to not use their system correctly anymore. In essence, they stop doing what got them to where they are at. They stop showing the business to qualified prospects and start managing their team. This always ends in disaster. Do you understand?"

Michael nodded his head and drew a deep breath. "Yes, I suppose I do."

Blake maintained eye contact for what seemed like an eternity. Michael felt as if the mentor was studying him. After a moment, he became uncomfortable and looked away.

"Does rejection still bother you?" the mentor asked.

Michael was embarrassed to admit it, but the truth was, yes, it did. That's why he found more comfort working with his team then he did in contacting new people. He watched as Blake turned his body and walked closer to the window. With his back to Michael, the mentor began to speak.

"Michael, if you or I show fifty people this business, what do you think we get paid for, the yeses or the nos?"

Blake's eyes remained fixed on the sea as he waited for a reply.

Michael answered carefully, "The yeses, I guess."

"The answer is neither," Blake corrected, before turning to face his student. "What you really get paid for is the fifty prospects. You see, there is no way to determine whether any of them will convert into sales." The mentor pulled a money clip out of his front pocket and removed ten one hundred dollar bills. He placed them on the table in front of Michael and spread them in a row like a handful of playing cards. Sitting down, he continued his lesson. "If I told you that you would earn $1,000 for every ten sales you make, but you had to take fifty prospects through our system before reaching those ten, the reality is, you really received that money for taking those prospects through the system, twenty dollars per prospect, to be specific, whether they were a yes or a no."

Blake reached down and slid two of the one hundred dollar bills away from the other eight. "In fact, if you multiply it out. You would really be getting paid $200 for the yes's and $800 for the no's. If you really wrap your brain around this, then you'd realize you get paid more for a no than you do for a yes. Do you know what this means?" Blake asked.

"I suppose I should be more excited about hearing the word no." Michael replied.

"Exactly!" Blake smiled. "What we're really talking about is the universally accepted 80/20 rule, which states, if you fail long enough, you will eventually succeed. You simply have to remember this is a numbers game, and all you have to do is continue to move the marbles."

Relationships

MICHAEL CONTEMPLATED the words spoken by the mentor, "If you fail long enough, you will eventually succeed." Those words caused him to think back to the poster of famous basketball legend, Michael Jordan, which credited him with the following quote:

I've missed more than 9,000 shots in my career. I've lost almost 300 games. 26 times, I've been trusted to take the game winning shot and missed. I've failed over and over and over again in my life. And that is why I succeed.

In theory, Blake's words made complete sense for Michael. But there was still one big obstacle to overcome. "I agree with you, but there's only one problem," Michael explained. "I've shown the business to the majority of the people on my list."

"And now you're mostly dealing with your cold market," Blake said, finishing Michael's thought.

"Exactly. How could I possibly find twenty quality prospects a month?"

"Quality contacts and potential customers are everywhere as long as a company has a product or service that adds value to a person's life, which ours does. You are offering time freedom and financial freedom as well as a wonderful product, correct?"

"Correct," Michael said.

"It goes back to what we talked about in my office. The best way to find customers is by building relationships, which is why those books I recommended are so important. People need to know you are honest and sincere. They need to know that if something is broken, you'll be there to fix it. They need to know they can trust and rely on you. Remember," Blake said, "People will not buy a membership to your company, unless they're confident in you. You have to be the difference maker. There are hundreds of direct selling companies out there. Some are terrific and some are not. You have to ask yourself, what separates my company from my competitors? The answer will always be—you."

"This is a valuable business principle that works in traditional business as well as in networking, isn't it?" Michael asked.

"All business is networking," Blake said. "There are more than one hundred and seventy thousand dentists in America. My cousin Ken is one of them. One day he was complaining about how bad business was. Now, an average visit to a dentist will cost a patient much less than $500. But the average American will spend more than twenty times that amount on dental visits over the course of a lifetime. I explained to Ken that when a person comes into his office he shouldn't just want to fill their cavity. As a business man, he should want that person to be the most satisfied customer in the world. I advised him to take time to get to know his customers, learn about their families and what they like to do in their down time. Send them postcards on their birthdays and holidays. Build a relationship and they will come back to him the next time."

"Did he take your advice?"

"He did, and his business increased by one-hundred and twenty percent within nine months. The referral rate was incredible." Blake looked Michael dead in the eye so the message was clear, "Don't be obsessed with making money. Be obsessed with adding value to someone else's life. That will make you a success in any career you choose, and don't stress out about finding twenty quality contacts a month. That's easy, you already know how to meet people, you just have to get out there in the right circles and do it."

"Do what, exactly?" Michael asked.

Blake shifted his head sideways, signaling for Michael to follow him. They walked through the crowded restaurant as the mentor continuously introduced Michael to others. He was impressed with Blake's ability to engage in seemingly effortless conversations. The mentor was in complete control and led the subject matter in any direction he wanted, which he usually did by asking questions and being sincerely interested in what people were saying to him.

Michael was also impressed with the amount of respect others had for Blake. This man was more than a financial success. He had mastered life. Michael was curious if the mentor was going to answer his question, but he had already learned that Blake was a strategist. He didn't do anything by chance. With that in mind, Michael waited, and just as he expected, Blake answered the question.

"An event like this would be a great place to prospect people, don't you agree?"

"Yes," Michael said.

"So do I, but when you're at a social gathering, you don't want to just walk up to a stranger and start talking about business, you want to talk about the most important subject to that stranger. The one they will be most interested to talk about, which is…"

"Themselves?" Michael said.

"Yes," Blake answered, "People don't care how much you know until they know how much you care. Have you ever heard the acronym FORM?"

"I have, isn't it an acronym that stands for family, occupation, and … I can't remember the other two."

"Recreation and money," Blake said.

"Yes. Family, occupation, recreation and money," Michael repeated.

"Those are the four things that people like to talk about when you engage them in conversation. The first three should be what you initially focus on."

Michael reflected back on the conversations that Blake just had with others and realized that the mentor did in fact ask people about their families and about recent recreational activities. Michael took note that the mentor was especially interested in listening when people talked about their vacations even though they were not traveling to the exotic places that Blake frequented. He also reflected upon his first conversation with Blake in his office at the Mercedes dealership. Within five minutes, Blake knew most of Michael's story. He knew about Michael's wife, his son, his job and more specific, he knew what Michael was trying to accomplish in life. It was all starting to make sense. Ask people about themselves and they will eventually tell you what they want out of life.

"I have to remember that," Michael said. True to his character, he reached into his coat pocket and took out a pen. Using a cocktail napkin as a pad, he quickly jotted down the word FORM. Then he placed the pen and napkin back in his pocket.

"FORM is a great way to initiate and lead a conversation, regardless of whether that person is a friend, acquaintance or cold contact. When you reach the point where the person you are speaking with tells you what they are interested in achieving, whether it be more money, more time, to retire early, or whatever else, I want you to remember one sentence that can open the door for you."

"I'm listening," Michael assured, as he tuned out the restaurant noise and concentrated solely on what Blake was teaching him.

"I may be able to help you accomplish that goal." Blake put his hand on Michael's shoulder again and looked him straight in the eyes. Every time the mentor did this Michael knew it was important that he understood the message. "Michael, I bet you can count on one finger how many times a person said that to you." He challenged before repeating the sentence, "I may be able to help you accomplish that goal."

"You're right," Michael said.

"It's the same with everyone else in this room. So the formula is simple; Listen to what a person is telling you. Find out what they want out of life. And let them know you have a solution. People will line up to follow you because you are the man who knows how to help them get what they want and they know you are genuinely interested in helping them achieve their dreams. From there, you will set the foundation for a relationship that will last a lifetime."

"You have spoken so much about developing relationships and the more time I spend with you, the more I understand what you are talking about. You have a unique way with the people in your life."

"I've always believed that a person can measure the quality of their life by the quality of their relationships and I also believe it's important to go out of my way to show that I value them. Remember Michael, people will forget the things you say and do, but they will never forget how you made them feel. When it comes right down to it, the quality of the relationships you form will be the glue that holds your team together."

"On that note," Michael said, "I have another question. As a leader, after I develop my team, what is the best method I can use to motivate them?"

"Throughout the years I have asked many people that same question and I've tried various different methods. I can emphatically tell you that the most effective way I have found to motivate my team, is through recognition. The more effort I put into showing how much I appreciate them, the more productive they are."

"My boss is the complete opposite. I can do a hundred things right and he never says a word, but the minute I make a mistake, he's all over me," Michael replied.

"Good, be grateful that you have that experience. Now you know what you don't want to be like. People may take a job for money, but if their boss doesn't show them any respect, they will never perform at their highest level. They'll work much harder when you praise and encourage them because those are basic human needs. If you don't provide some form of recognition for your team members, they'll leave and go work for someone who does, even if it means making less money."

"When and how have you recognized people for their efforts?" Michael asked.

"I prefer to do it in person and in front of others. Each week we had presentations that we opened up to all of our team and their guests. During the presentation, we'd talk about the levels that certain individuals had achieved up to that point and the levels beyond where they currently were. I would ask people to stand so we could applaud them for achieving those levels. Those who had achieved higher levels of recognition, I would ask to come up to the front of the room and share who they were, what they did for a living, and why they were excited about the business."

"We have been doing the same thing at our presentations," Michael said, "And I have to admit, one of my early goals was to reach a level where I would be asked to stand up and share those things with the people in the room."

"It makes you feel good, right?" Blake said.

"Yes, it does."

"Laura and I would also have team building sessions at our home. Any time we had individuals or teams in the room who had achieved something worthwhile, the entire room would give them a standing ovation. It's a simple gesture, easy to do, but the end result is a much deserved pat on the back and an overall increase in morale. Then, of course, we also held monthly events, where people from throughout the region would get together for training and to celebrate the successes and achievements of our colleagues. As you know, our company also sends out a quarterly newsletter naming all the people who have reached the higher levels in our business, enabling them to share some of their story and share a nugget or two on how people could enhance their own personal performances. I started that newsletter ten years ago, when I was the head of our training division."

"You really put a lot of effort into recognizing others," Michael said.

"It's necessary. They're my team. They worked hard to achieve their dreams and as a result they help me achieve mine. I'd be crazy to dismiss that fact. Recognition is vital, but to be effective it must be positive, sincere and timely. I read an article in *USA Today* several years ago that stated the two most underused words in corporate America are 'thank you.'"

"That's a shame."

"It sure is. If you want to develop a productive team with positive energy, run promotions, encourage those who are working hard, and provide public recognition for people who achieve specific levels of success. People will not only feel appreciated, they're likely to go out and do it again."

"The fact that you do all of this is just another reason why people respect you so much."

Blake put his arm around Michael, "You are a young man with big dreams. You want the yacht, the sports cars, and the mansion, but the average person just wants to become debt-free. If you help enough people pay off their credit cards, get out of debt and earn enough money to take a vacation, you'll have the yacht and the sports cars and the mansion. It's like Zig Ziglar says, 'You will get all you want in life if you help enough other people get what they want.'"

Blake and Michael continued to engage in meaningful conversations with others. Michael paid close attention to the words that came out of the mentor's mouth. Interestingly, Blake rarely talked about himself, he just asked questions and absorbed what other people were saying. As Michael observed, it became obvious that everyone at the party delighted in talking about themselves. Curiously, more than one person remarked about how much they enjoyed their brief conversation with the mentor, regardless of the fact that Blake hardly said a word about himself. He just kept asking other people questions about themselves and listening.

Overcoming Obstacles

THE OUTDOOR SEATING deck of the restaurant was empty. This was partly because of the drop in temperature after the sunset, but mainly because everyone was enjoying the party, especially Michael and Kristen, who were sitting at a table with their hosts, the Easton's.

Over the past hour, Michael had been craving something. Although it may seem strange to others, he wanted to spend just one minute on the balcony, doing one of his favorite activities, listening to the sound of ocean waves crashing. Michael excused himself and stepped outside onto the seating deck. He leaned on the balcony railing, took a deep breath and closed his eyes. A cold, refreshing breeze blew onto his face, carrying the scent of the ocean.

"I want this," he said softly to himself.

Michael wasn't referring to anything material. He was referencing something much more valuable, the feeling he had when his stress seemed to disappear. For some reason, that is exactly what happened every time he was near the ocean.

"I really want this," he repeated.

From the darkness behind him, a voice replied, "Then you shall have it."

The response startled Michael, who thought he was alone. He turned to see a man in his early thirties emerge from the shadow.

Embarrassed, he said, "I'm sorry, I didn't know anyone else was out here."

"Don't apologize. I relate to your passion." The man reached out his hand, "Hi, I'm Grey Daniels." They shook hands.

Michael didn't recognize the face or the voice, but he certainly knew the name. Grey Daniels life was one of the most celebrated rags-to-riches stories in the industry. As a young man, Grey had connected with the wrong crowd and instead of getting involved in sports or other constructive activities, he experimented with drugs. It was so bad that before he turned twenty-one, Grey was an addict.

Michael knew from the stories that others told him that Grey was never prospected for the business. One night, he was hanging out in front of a convenience store when he overheard one man talking to a prospect about network marketing. The prospect blew the man off, but Grey approached him and asked, "Is the business you are talking about something that I could do?"

As legend has it, the man replied, "I doubt it." Before leaving, the man wrote the time and location of their next hotel presentation on a piece of paper and handed it to Grey saying, "But if you want to take a look, be here at this time."

Grey went to the meeting two days later. He sat in the back row and watched the presentation. The man who invited him, however, did not show. Grey didn't own nice clothing, so he wore a flannel shirt and jeans with rips on both knees. He looked, and smelled, like a kid who was in desperate need of a bath. No one paid attention to him. They actually went out of their way to ignore him. What the others didn't know, was that Grey's best friend had recently passed away—the result of reckless choices. That was a wakeup call for the kid, who knew he had to change, but was desperate for options. He was also desperate for guidance, but on that night, no one offered any.

Grey showed up the next week and sat in on the presentation again, this time, in the front row. Afterward, he walked up to several people—seven to be exact—and asked them if they could get him started. All seven declined. Grey wasn't the type of person to give up. When he made a decision, he followed through, good or bad. He was stubborn that way. Lucky for him, the eighth couple he approached had a strong religious background and believed that everyone was capable of changing and no one should be denied a second chance.

Grey didn't know many people. Those he did know weren't the type of people you'd want to develop a business with. Some said he randomly called people out of the phone book and said, "You don't know me, my name is Grey Daniels, but I am looking for a few key people in your neighborhood who wouldn't be opposed to earning additional income. Do you ever look at ways of diversifying? If not, do you know anybody who does?"

Even though Grey had no credibility, he reached the top of his company in less than four years because he had one thing that trumped his circumstances—heart of a champion.

A chance meeting with Grey Daniels was a treat for Michael.

"I heard about you," Michael said.

"I get nervous every time someone says that," Grey joked.

"Seriously, I found your story to be very inspirational."

"Thank you. I heard about you too. You're the new guy that Blake's working with, Michael, right?"

How could this man possibly know about me? Michael wondered. *He's a top achiever, a legend; and I'm really just getting started.* His thoughts reverted back to when Blake told him that others take notice of new team members who do the right activities. "Yes," he said, "Michael Harper."

A million questions ran through Michael's head. What could he ask a man who had succeeded against all odds? Before he could say anything, there was a knock on the glass window. It was Kristen, motioning for Michael to come back in because dinner was being served. He held up his finger to signify that he would be there in one minute, then turned back to Grey and asked, "How did you do it?"

"Do what?" Grey asked.

"Overcome so much to build the business as big as you did."

Grey laughed. In his eyes he didn't do anything more than any other top money earner did. "Michael, don't be one of those people who think circumstances are there to hold you back. Research some of the most successful and influential people in history and you will discover that each of them had their own bag of hammers to carry. If you could exchange the challenges you have in your life for those that others are faced with, you would probably be better off keeping your own." Then he summed up by saying, "If you want something bad enough, you will have it. As long as you never let your circumstances or emotions affect your passion or performance."

"Your attitude is inspiring."

"Thank you, Michael. I have come to the conclusion that the greatest discovery a human being can make is that he can alter his life by altering his attitude."

The last six months of Michael's life provided him with enough personal experience to validate that comment.

Grey patted Michael on the back and handed him his business card, "Call me if there's anything I could do to help you, and get in there before your food gets cold." Then he disappeared back into the crowded restaurant.

Michael returned to his wife and enjoyed a spectacular dinner. The couple sampled the bistro's most popular dishes, which included Alaskan king crab legs, yellow fin Tuna Nicoise and Steak Au Poivre. For desert, Michael had raspberry sorbet and Kristen chose her favorite, crème brûlée, neither disappointed.

After desert, Michael was standing near Blake when a pleasant and stylishly dressed middle-aged woman approached the mentor with her hand extended, "Hello Blake."

"Hello Gabby." Blake clasped her hand in between both of his.

"The party is wonderful," she said.

"I'm glad you are enjoying yourself. Is Phil here? I haven't seen him yet and I'd like to say hello."

Gabby's smile faded, "No, he couldn't make it. His company is restructuring and he's been under a lot of stress lately."

"Will the change affect your family?" Blake asked bluntly.

"I sure hope not. Some of his co-workers were unexpectedly let go last week. One of them worked there for twenty-seven years."

"Wow, I'm sorry to hear that," Blake replied, with obvious concern. He motioned toward Michael "Gabby, I want you to meet my friend, Michael Harper."

On Blake's signal, Michael stepped forward.

"It's nice to meet you, Michael," she said.

"The pleasure is all mine, Gabby."

Blake continued with the introduction, "Gabby and Phil are friends of ours from years ago. We lost touch, but recently reconnected when we bumped into each other at the airport." He then turned to Gabby and said, "Michael and his wife Kristen have just joined my company. They are in the business of helping people dig their financial well, so to speak."

Michael was impressed with the colorful introduction, especially because of the response that came from it.

"Financial well?" Gabby replied.

"You see how fickle the economy is today. More people than ever before are looking to diversify their income for protection, or as I say, dig their financial well before they need the water." Blake said.

Gabby's eyebrows raised. She was obviously interested in hearing more.

"Since were on the topic," Blake continued, "If you and Phil are open to looking for a way to earn an additional income on a part-time basis, you owe it to yourself to take a look at our business model. I believe Michael and Kristen can help you accomplish your financial goals."

"That would be wonderful," Gabby replied. "What exactly would it entail?" she asked.

Before Michael could answer, Blake replied with, "I'm sure Michael can get all your questions answered tomorrow Gabby, but tonight I want you to enjoy yourself. Why don't you and Michael exchange numbers. Let him know when the best time to contact you would be, preferably when Phil is home so he can listen in as well. I think with Phil's drive and your business savvy, you would both do very well."

"Terrific," Gabby enthusiastically replied as she wrote her home number on back of a business card and handed it to Michael. "We'll both be home tomorrow evening after seven."

"Great, I'll call you around 7:30 with some information."

"I'll be looking forward to that," Gabby said. She turned her attention back to Blake. "Thank you, Blake. I'm happy I said something. I believe things happen for a reason."

"We all do," Blake replied. "Now let's enjoy the rest of the party."

After Gabby walked away, Blake turned to Michael, "Does that validate what we were talking about earlier?"

"Yes it does. You just have to ask people about themselves and the opening will present itself."

"Exactly, you are learning, young man," said the mentor.

"You also created curiosity without saying too much about what we do." Michael said.

"That's right, it's too early to get into details. She needs exposures. Plus, her husband isn't here to listen. Why do something twice if you only have to do it once to get the results you desire," Blake replied.

"I think I should start calling you Yoda."

Blake found humor in the comment, "By the way, Gabby is the one you really want to be in business with. She can do anything her husband can do only backwards and wearing high heels," Blake said with a smile.

Michael was curious, "Blake, if she's a friend of yours, why didn't you show her the business?"

"As I said, we lost touch for years and by the time we reconnected, Laura and I had transitioned from developing our own team to mentoring and training leaders in the industry, and although the four of us had consistently tried to get together socially, something always seemed to come up. Truth be told, that was the longest conversation we had since that day at the airport."

"She obviously still respects you."

"And I respect her. I respect my friends and team members and I expect the same respect in return. Unfortunately, that's not always the case." The mentor was quiet for a moment, distracted by a man who was at the bar talking with others, perhaps the man had a drink or two more than he should have. Michael's eyes followed Blake's gaze. The man seemed out of place and did not carry himself with the class that the others in the room did. After a moment of silence, he spoke up.

"Blake?"

"Do you see that man over there?" Blake asked, motioning with his head.

"Yes. What about him?"

"He is planning to leave one of my companies and go to work for a competitor."

"How do you know that?"

"Let's just say you don't get to where I am without a certain awareness of what's happening around you," Blake replied.

Michael's eyes were fixed on the man. "What are you going to do?"

"Nothing." Blake said, shrugging it off.

Michael looked at Blake, perplexed. "Nothing? Aren't you afraid he is going to hurt your business, maybe take others with him?"

Blake looked at Michael, "If you intend to succeed at anything you are going to have to understand that paranoia and success cannot coexist. I can't stop that man from going where he wants to go, nor would I want to. He is free to do what he feels is right for him and his family, but I also realize that he will bring his habits with him. He's not a key player or top producer in my company and he will not be a top producer for my competition. He'll just find himself in a position where he has to start over only to discover the grass wasn't greener on the other side of the fence. All he really had to do was water and fertilize his own lawn and he would have done exceptionally well right where he was. You see Michael, the problem with leaving is you have to take yourself with you. It's his loss, but I wish him luck."

"You don't feel betrayed?"

"Sometimes people disappoint," Blake explained, "Someone who trusts can never be betrayed, only mistaken. It's difficult to predict what some people are going to do, but it's important to choose who you associate with very carefully because those who are closest to you will play a big part in your level of success."

"Speaking of association, Kristen and I registered for the convention in Orlando next month."

"I know," Blake replied.

"You do?"

"Yes, I asked Denise from the convention planning company to let me know when your registration came in."

"How did you know I was going to register?"

"Why wouldn't you? That's where the leaders are going to be, and if you intend to be a leader, that's where you need to be. Association with like-minded people is an essential ingredient of success and learning from a variety of people who have accomplished what you are striving to accomplish is another form of personal growth. If you are determined to win, you have to surround yourself with winners. Listening to audios from top achievers is important, but you already learned on my yacht that it's entirely different to press the palms of those people and learn industry secrets as you share a cup of coffee with them. You may know *of* them, but you don't know them and they don't know you. In order to build a successful partnership, you need to figure out a way to spend time with the people you admire," Blake replied.

"At first, I was a little concerned with the cost of the trip, but once we registered, my commitment level increased a little more and I set the goal to make enough money in one month to cover the expenses. We achieved our goal in three weeks." Michael said.

"That's great. Many of your teammates will encounter that same obstacle when you promote events like this to them, but you have to let them know it's a mistake to put a price on self-education. I used to tell others not to think about how much it will cost to go, instead, I would urge them to think about what it would cost them not to go. Every top producer I know in any line of work attends conferences and events that are designed to help them advance their business or careers to the next level. That's why they're top producers. I would go as far as to say, if you don't go, you won't grow."

"I understand. Kristen and I are excited about the event."

"Speaking of Kristen, where are the girls?" Blake asked, as he scanned the crowded restaurant.

Michael spotted them sitting down at a nearby table, laughing, of course. The four of them regrouped.

"Laura, do you have it?" Blake asked.

"I sure do," his wife replied. She reached into her purse, pulled out an envelope and handed it to Kristen.

"What's this?" Kristen asked.

"Just a little anniversary gift for the two of you," Laura replied.

Michael and Kristen did not expect the gesture. "How did you know it was our anniversary," he asked.

"When you came to my office you mentioned that you were married in December. We weren't sure of the date, but we knew we were going to see you tonight," Blake explained, "Go ahead open it."

Kristen opened the envelope, which revealed two full treatment gift certificates to a luxurious day spa in Pennsylvania. Her reaction was priceless, "Oh my, you didn't have to do this."

"We wanted too," Laura replied, "Believe me when I tell you, it's possible to do nothing for an entire day and feel like it's the best day of your life. You're going to love it there."

"We don't know how to thank you," Kristen said.

"Don't thank us," Blake responded, "Just enjoy yourselves."

Michael and Kristen had a wonderful evening at the Avenue restaurant. They were disappointed when the party ended, but they were excited to get home to Dylan. On the drive home, Michael told Kristen about the conversations he had with Blake as well as the one he had with Grey Daniels on the outdoor sitting deck. They agreed to work harder in promoting the

Orlando convention to their team members. It was a smart move. After learning of their commitment, many of the others became encouraged, enough to get off the fence and attend with them. This made Michael realize that people really were watching, and duplicating every move he made.

23

The Atmosphere of Expectancy

MICHAEL AND KRISTEN could hear the faint sounds of music, cheers and applause from outside the convention hall in Orlando. As they approached, the sound increased with each step. The moment they entered the convention room, the couple knew they had made the right decision.

Thousands of excited people mingled as the patriotic music filled the air. Michael quickly noted two gigantic video screens hanging from the ceiling. They bordered both sides of the stage, which brought the audience closer to the action. Energy filled in the room. It felt as if they had just walked into a concert. They knew they were there to be educated and inspired, not just entertained. Their arrival was timely because the first speaker was about to take the stage. Michael and Kristen were not sure where their teammates were so they settled into the only two empty seats they could find, near the back of the room.

The stage was gracefully decorated with greenery and a single glass podium in the center. A handsome couple stood behind it.

Tapping on his wife's arm Michael leaned in and whispered, "That's Richard and Dawn Parker, one of the couples I met on Blake's yacht."

From stage, the couple enthusiastically introduced the first speaker. She was a single woman in her late-forties and she had built one of the largest organizations in the company. Michael was excited because he had just listened to one of her audios the week before. The crowd stood and gave her a thundering applause when she took the stage. She wore an expensive form-fitting navy blue and white ensemble and a power-exuding jacket. Her posture displayed poise and confidence.

The applause continued as the camera scanned the audience. Michael fixed his eyes on one of the big screens. He recognized some of the faces of people in attendance from a recent issue of *Success from Home* magazine. He couldn't believe he was in the same room with people who have achieved such a high level of success. Just being in their presence gave Michael and Kristen a greater belief that they were going to accomplish their goals. It took a few minutes before the applause faded and the speaker was able to persuade the audience to settle back into their seats.

Once she began to speak, Michael was amazed how quickly silence had blanketed the convention hall. There was no sound in the room other than her amplified voice and she commanded and captured the audience's attention with ease. Both he and Kristen were immersed in the woman's speech, which focused on the many challenges she had to overcome in order to achieve such a high level of success. Her talk was reminiscent of Blake's lesson on perseverance and was only the first of many great talks that followed.

The training Michael and Kristen received from all of the speakers was priceless. They learned effective contacting and promoting techniques, and how to overcome objections. Michael was introduced to the '*Feel, Felt, Found*' technique. He took detailed notes and practiced how he would answer the next time someone tried to tell him something like *nobody makes money in these things*. His response to that objection would begin with, *I know how you feel, I felt the same way, but last week I attended an event in Orlando and let me share with you what I found out …*

He also learned that when people say they don't have time or money he should ask them if they'd like to change that. One speaker also assured the audience that when it comes to prospecting, a networker can't say the wrong thing to the right person and they also can't say the right thing to the wrong person. The thought of this gave Michael comfort because he had been putting unnecessary stress on himself when it came to trying to do everything right.

The speakers reinforced that building a business was a numbers game and although there were always ways to improve, the most important thing he could do is take action and remain consistent day in and day out. By doing so, he would improve his technique in the process. These were not foreign lessons that he was learning. Blake had been saying everything he heard from stage since the day he agreed to take Michael under his wings. Nevertheless, sometimes a person needs to hear a message multiple times, from various people before it sinks in.

When Michael and Kristen left the convention hall, they entered another room that featured a full product and services display and realized their company offered much more than they were even aware of. In that room, they also had the chance to meet some of the people on the corporate staff, as well as more of the leaders of the company. Michael and Kristen, along with their teammates, enjoyed this time because they were able to receive guidance and tips on some of the situations they were personally encountering. This one-on-one time with leaders was known as the meeting after the meeting. In many ways, Michael found this time to be even more valuable than that which he spent in the convention hall.

On the following day, they returned to the convention for more powerful training on leadership and team building. When it came time for recognition, Michael and Kristen crossed the stage for the levels they had achieved. Michael's heart was beating out of his chest when he stepped up to the microphone. He was asked to say his name and where he was from, but he was so nervous that he had almost forgotten both. Lucky for him that was all he was expected to share with the massive crowd. When everyone cheered their accomplishment, Kristen turned to Michael and jokingly said, "That's the same way they cheer for us at our jobs every day."

As higher levels were recognized, the couple watched in awe as a seemingly endless line of people crossed on stage. Smaller teams of people gathered in front of the stage to cheer for people they knew and worked with. It was an awesome display of reward and recognition, just the way Blake described it to be.

The higher the level of achievement within the company, the more time that person or couple was given to share from stage. Listening to their stories provided great inspiration. The struggles and challenges that some of them had overcome were greater than the ones he and Kristen were facing. One couple had filed for bankruptcy two years earlier and was now making more money every month than they were every year in their previous corporate careers. He realized that people are like sticks of dynamite, they have great power on the inside, but nothing happens until the fuse is lit. The people crossing the stage at the higher levels were evidence of that.

One of the achievers shared a phrase with the crowd that Michael felt was directed to him personally. The man said, "A leader of one may one day become a leader of many, but if you can't lead one you'll never lead any." Michael needed to hear that. He had been secretly hoping for a leader to appear on his team and set the pace for the others to follow, but the moment he heard those words, he realized that *he* needed to become that leader.

Right there and then, Michael had made the decision that he would never miss an event because the words spoken could propel his business. He knew he couldn't bottle the energy in the convention hall and bring it home to share it with others, so he committed to become an expert promoter and bring a freshman class with him to all future business related events. He knew others needed to experience this for themselves. It was obvious that he would find his teammates in the living rooms, but his leaders would emerge from the ballrooms and convention halls.

The event fully enabled Michael to understand the importance of association. Being in Orlando, experiencing the positive energy, and seeing all the people who were having success with his company provided him with a higher level of belief in himself and his company. That belief ultimately resulted in raised expectations and an increase of passion and purpose. His overall vision had become enlarged and as a couple, Michael and Kristen realized with one hundred percent certainty that they had made the right choice for their family.

They returned from Orlando with a new perspective. The words they said were the same as before. But now those words seemed to take on a greater meaning. At the event, Michael and Kristen connected with more high achievers who expressed interest in working with them. After returning home, they called on those team members often and continued to move in the direction of their dreams.

The three months that followed were better than Michael could have ever imagined they would be. He was applying every principle he learned from Blake and the other leaders in the business. He was counseling daily with Blake and he was regularly moving the marbles from the prospect jar to the presentation jar.

While driving his car, Michael played his CD's, listened to inspirational stories and imagined being on stage with Kristin, telling their own story to the massive crowd. The thought of inspiring others added fuel to his fire.

In addition to the increased income that he and his wife were now earning, another fringe benefit came along with the education and experience that Michael had been receiving. He became so good at dealing with problems and working with others that his boss began to take notice of his change in attitude. He began to stand out from the others at work, who still resorted to criticizing others and complaining about how bad things were. Michael never complained at work. He willingly accepted every task assigned to him and completed that task better than anyone, even his boss, could have expected. He quickly became the bosses go-to guy, and when a promotional opportunity unexpectedly opened up, Michael's work ethic and attitude trumped the seniority of his coworkers and he became their new foreman. This new position provided him with better hours, and more money, but did not distract him from consistently working his business, which he knew was the only way he was going to achieve his true dreams and goals.

He continued to work full-time on his job, and part-time on his fortune.

24

It's Worth It

TWO MORE MONTHS had passed, and Michael and Kristen were excited to finally have the opportunity to take advantage of the anniversary gift they received from Blake and Laura. It was June, which also meant they had been with the company for twelve months. A trip to the spa was a nice way to celebrate that achievement as well.

Needless to say, the couple was excited to spend a relaxing day at the award-winning spa located in a luxury resort called *The Lodge at Woodloch*. Summer was the perfect time of year for a two-hour drive, part of which was through the Pocono's in Pennsylvania. The mountain foliage was alive and dancing with color. Deer were everywhere. At one point, they spotted an eagle and pulled off the road so they could watch the majestic bird fly. The *Lodge at Woodloch* was listed as one of the Top Ten destination spas in the world by *Travel and Leisure* magazine. It was a private lakefront resort that included 75 acres of woodland gardens and a private championship golf course.

When they arrived at the security gate, they were eager to see and experience the crowned resort. The security guard reviewed his list and directed them toward the lodge. Everything Michael and Kristen had heard and read about the resort had not prepared them for the architectural beauty.

The exterior of the lodge was magnificent, featuring large wooden columns, a stone foundation and earth inspired accents. The lodge structure itself appeared to be a continuation of nature, breathtaking in every way possible. They were greeted by a valet and directed down a covered walkway into the main entrance.

The inside of the lodge was inspired by the outdoors. It was as if they walked through doors and right back out into a natural conservation. The oversized windows perfectly framed breathtaking glances of outdoor vistas. It was like looking at a moving painting as the birds flew by and the paddlers slowly moved across the lake. Throughout the lodge were terraces and porches that opened and invited them to stroll around ponds and gardens. The steam from the hot tubs completed the magical effect of a luxury and nature combination that seamlessly flowed inside and outside of the retreat.

Michael and Kristen called in advance to set up their personalized spa experience by choosing from a series of unique facial and body treatment selections. Their host was waiting at the front desk to meet them and hand them their itinerary. They began their day with native stone massages. The treatment consisted of warmed and scented oil-soaked basalt stones placed on their bodies and incorporated with classic Swedish massage techniques. This provided a level of relaxation neither of them had previously experienced.

After their massages, Michael enjoyed a half-hour in the hot tub. Although the scenery was beautiful, he closed his eyes and cleared his mind of all of life's stresses. Kristen enjoyed a European deep-cleansing facial, which allowed her to do the same. After their private sessions, they reconnected for an intimate lunch at the Lodges world-renowned restaurant, *Tree*. The choice of the restaurant's name became obvious when they entered the dining area, which appeared as if it was perched in a tree. Kristen chose a delectable teriyaki salmon dish that melted in her mouth. Michael decided upon the roasted lobster with basil risotto. It was beyond delicious.

After lunch, they took a relaxing walk through a one-mile paved nature trail and enjoyed the views of exotic flowers and the pristine lake. The experience totally rehabilitated them physically, mentally and spiritually. They agreed to make their visit to the spa an annual tradition.

Taking time to reward each other for the efforts they had been putting into their business was a great way for the couple to rejuvenate. On the way home, Kristen told Michael about some of the challenges she was having at work. They were nothing out of the ordinary, but as he listened to his wife speak, Michael suddenly realized that over the past three months, the couple had earned more in their part-time business than Kristen did as a teacher.

"What do you think it would take for us to bring you home from work?" he asked.

"You mean, for good?"

"Yes."

Kristen bit her lower lip the way she always did when pondering something, "I don't know. I suppose we should wait until we are making three times my income. What do you think?"

"I think that's a great goal," he answered.

Over the next hour and a half, they strategized and formulated a game plan to make it happen. Since they were already halfway to their goal, the couple decided that eleven months would give them more than enough time to reach it. They set the goal to retire Kristen at the end of the upcoming school year, in June.

Michael and Kristen went to work, and they quickly realized that challenges and struggles don't simply go away just because a person's commitment level grows. They also learned that by keeping their eyes on their goal, those challenges and struggles seemed far less threatening then they would if they approached their goal haphazardly.

There simply was no obstacle great enough to stop them. Any time a member of their team had a no-show, they would call that person and say, "Nothing matters when the dream is big enough." If a new person with promise quit the business, they would call the person who brought them in and say, "Nothing matters when the dream is big enough." Whatever the problem, they would always respond with, "Nothing matters when the dream is big enough."

The dream for them was to bring Kristen home from work. Nothing was going to prevent them from making that dream a reality. They had eleven months to attain their goal. They reached it in four. After counseling with Blake and Laura, they planned Kristen's retirement party.

Kristen knew that Michael was going to be waiting for her in the school's parking lot on her final day of work. What she didn't know was that Michael rented a silver stretch limousine. Inside he had champagne, two dozen roses and a gift he had purchased several weeks ago. It was sitting in a large gift bag with a pink ribbon on top, Kristen's favorite color.

When the bell rang, students began to pour out of the school. They were curious to see who was in the limo. Not Kristen, the moment she saw the car, she knew.

Michael stepped out with the roses in his hand and waited for his sweetheart to approach. He could see the tears in her eyes, which were a combination of happiness and sorrow. They embraced, and some of the other teachers, many of which were already on their team, applauded. This moment was a reality for Kristen, but a dream building session for the others.

In the limo, after toasting their achievement, Michael handed his wife the gift bag. Her emotions got the better of her when she discovered her dream Coach bag was inside.

"We have to take it off the dream board now," Kristen said.

"Definitely," Michael said.

When they arrived back home, a group of their team members were waiting at the house to celebrate. The party was not just a celebration of Kristen's freedom—it was a celebration of the fact that one of them had made it. Hearing that this little home-based business can set a person free is one thing, but seeing someone do it before your eyes is something different all together.

The next evening, Michael and Kristen had dinner in New York City and capped the night off with a Broadway show. While sitting in the theater, Michael reminisced back to several months earlier when he contemplated whether or not the rewards were going to be worth the struggle. He smiled, because when he looked into his wife's eyes and saw that sparkle reappear, he didn't think about the no shows or the critics. Looking back, the challenges he encountered didn't seem all that big anymore.

Were the rewards worth the struggles he had to go through? The answer was a resounding yes.

Although bringing Kristen home was their goal, leaving her teaching job was not an easy decision. She loved working with the kids, but the rewards that came with being able to raise Dylan was far greater than either of them could ever anticipate. The decision came at a perfect time because the same month Kristen retired, they found out they were expecting another child.

Burn the Boats

It WAS A CLEAR morning and signs of spring were appearing. A few months had passed since Kristen retired from teaching and the business was booming. She was pregnant and Dylan was now 2 ½ years old. Michael had been working the business consistently. On this particular morning, he was driving through Sea Bright on his way to meet a prospect for lunch. He left his home thirty minutes earlier than he had to because he wanted to stop by and see Blake, who was preparing to take an extended vacation on his yacht. He wasn't sure what time the mentor was casting off, so when Michael arrived, it pleased him to see that the yacht was still docked.

As he pulled in to the lot, he spotted Blake exiting his car. He pulled up and stepped out to talk with him.

"I'm glad I caught you before you left," Michael said.

"Hey Michael, what a surprise," the mentor replied.

"So, where are you going?" Michael asked.

"We're heading to St. Barts, then Virgin Gorda and possibly some time in the Grenadines. We're keeping our options open."

"Wow, sounds great. How long do you plan to be away?"

"We've been away. We're just heading back home," Blake corrected, with his signature smile. "We'll be gone for two or three months,"

"Good for you."

"What brings you down?" Blake asked.

"I'm meeting with a prospect in the area. I had a few minutes so I wanted to stop by and thank you for everything."

Blake proudly looked over Michael. It was clear that the mentor was very pleased with the man he had become. "You have done a tremendous job with the business Michael."

"I couldn't have done it without your help, Blake," Michael answered.

"Nonsense, you've always been sitting on oil, remember?"

"Yes, I remember."

"You know Michael, when you came aboard, your goals and dreams were practically non-existent. It took time to get you back to where you could dream again."

"I know."

"Now that you've reached them, and your business is growing, what's next?"

Michael put his arm on Blake's shoulder the way the mentor used to do to him when they first met. "You know, I've been thinking a lot about that myself," he began, "You have a gorgeous trophy in your office."

Michael was obviously referring to the Top Achiever Eagle Award that Blake proudly displayed in the corner of his home office.

"Yes, I do," the mentor replied.

"I was wondering what I would have to do to get one of those."

Blake didn't respond initially. He quickly reflected upon the hundreds of people he had counseled and trained over the years in the network marketing industry that have made a similar comment. Making money in the industry is something anyone could do, reaching the top levels requires sacrifice, but becoming a top achiever requires something else altogether. He knew Michael had the education, talent and desire to make it to the top, but would he have the one missing ingredient?

"That's a big goal, Michael, and big goals require big commitments." Blake said.

"I'm up for the challenge," Michael said.

"Fantastic. If that's the case, there's only one thing left for you to do," Blake said.

"What's that?"

"Burn the boats," Blake answered.

Michael didn't understand. "Do what?"

"Have you ever heard the name Hernando Cortez?"

"No."

"Hernando Cortez was a Spanish conquistador who, in 1519, assembled an army of 500 and set out to take the world's richest treasure that had been held by the Aztec Empire for six hundred years. Army after army had tried to take this treasure, but they all failed because the natives outnumbered and out fought all the other armies. Cortez knew what he was up against and he knew the natural instinct of his army. He knew that when they landed and realized they were severely outnumbered and outmatched they would try to retreat to the boats. He needed to make their level of commitment beyond that which the others who tried before him had."

"What did he do?" Michael asked.

"Instead of jumping on the boats, arriving at Veracruz and attacking, Cortez took time to talk to his army about their life and what the lives of the generations to follow were going to be like after they took the treasure. He helped cultivate the dream and inspire them before they even set sail."

"Smart move," Michael acknowledged.

"Yes, but half way through their voyage doubt and fear began to spread throughout the ship and Cortez could sense the reluctance of his soldiers. So when they landed near the site of Veracruz, he gathered his army on the day of the battle. I'm sure they expected a strategic talk, maybe a motivational speech but Cortez knew that would not be enough. Instead he turned to men with torches and said three words."

"Burn the boats," Michael said.

"That's correct. When all eleven ships were burned to prevent any thought of retreat, the message was crystal clear, if they were going home. They weren't going home on their boats."

"Wow, that's a serious commitment. Take the treasure or die," Michael said.

"It sure was. And an amazing thing happened as a result of that commitment, Cortez and his army defeated and conquered the Aztec Empire and they took the treasure. Cortez knew that life shrinks or expands in proportion of one's courage. That day, his army accomplished what no other had been able to."

"That's an amazing story," Michael said.

"Big goals require big commitments," Blake repeated, "The question for you becomes, what is the thing in your life that is keeping you from getting what you say you want? What are the boats that you need to burn?"

Michael contemplated the question before admitting, "For me, I think it was always the fear of failure, or the fear of being criticized when trying to break away from the pack. Those were two things that used to prevent me from pursuing my dreams."

"Once you completely burn the boats you can go and take what's rightfully yours." Blake said. "This is your life, Michael. This is not a dress rehearsal. When you're gone, people will summarize your life in one sentence. What do you want that sentence to be? Whatever you do, don't let someone else pick it for you."

There was an intense moment before Blake continued with what would turn out to be his final lesson before departing. "You've come a long way, Michael. By now you've realized that in our industry, if you aren't getting the results you want you're either doing the wrong things, or not enough of the right things. You're obviously doing the right things, now you need to develop an urgency mindset. You do know that running as hard as you can for an extended period of time is the only thing you haven't done, right?"

Michael nodded. He understood what Blake was getting at. After the time he spent on the yacht, he ran 100 miles per hour for a couple weeks. He did the same after attending regional events and the convention in Orlando, but after running for a period of time, he would always stop to take a break in one way, shape or form. He never stopped building the business. He only stopped doing the activities that made the business grow the fastest.

Michael listened intently as the mentor continued, "Anyone I know that has achieved a significant level of success in this or any industry has displayed an urgency mindset for an extended period of time. I can say with one-hundred percent certainty that any leader in the direct selling industry would agree that urgency is the missing ingredient in the majority of individuals and organizations that fail. Urgency," Blake stressed, "or the lack thereof, affects everything, especially the emotional side of business."

"Why is that exactly?" Michael asked.

"The speed at which you pursue your goals affects everything," Blake explained. "Don't ask me how or why, but people can sense when you have an urgency mindset. When you possess true urgency, your prospect will feel compelled to be a part of your plan, and even if they don't buy your product, they may refer you to someone that will, and may possibly become a customer at a later time. Nevertheless, they will have felt the power of urgency from someone with purpose. Urgency has an almost mystical ability to become a magnetic force for you that will enable you to attract the success you're looking for."

"What are some of the things I could do to further develop that mindset?"

"First, put yourself in a frame of mind that the people you know and meet are going to get in business with someone else if you don't show them first. Next, fill your calendar with back-to-back meetings. If you schedule six meetings, you're a totally different person than if you schedule only one. With six, you don't care if the prospect signs up. You want to get the job done and get to the next meeting. People will sense that and will recognize the fact that you don't need them. When you schedule only one meeting, you become desperate for results. Scheduling six in a week will help you cross-over an emotional hurdle. The most powerful word in any sales related industry is the word, *next*. When you stop caring what everyone thinks, your business will explode. And Michael, don't ask me how or why because I don't know, but people can tell how fast you're pursuing your goals. When you compress more work in a shorter amount of time and the speed at which you pursue your goals is intensified, you'll achieve results faster and end up creating momentum."

"Keep the bases loaded and when I get a hit, someone's coming home," Michael summarized.

"Exactly. Nice analogy," Blake said. "And I'll tell you another fact that most people never realize. The less urgent you are, the more painful things become. Working with one or two prospects at a time almost always ends in failure. People with no urgency have no game plan and have not clearly defined their dream. As a result, they end up living a life of regret."

"Like so many others," Michael replied.

"Like *too* many others," Blake corrected. "The next ninety days can set you on a whole new path. Develop a game plan and begin a ninety-day run. After those ninety days are up, do it again. With urgency—you're a man on a mission. Without it—you're just a nice guy."

Blake looked at his watch. Michael knew the mentor had to go, so he began the farewell process. "Blake, thank you so much for all that you have done for me. I hope to someday repay you."

"Stay on this journey. That's all I want from you." Blake reached out his right arm and placed his hand on Michael's left shoulder before continuing. "You know Michael. I'm not going anywhere, but I can't bring you much further. I taught you everything I know."

"I understand," Michael said. "Thank you, Blake."

The mentor gave an approving nod. It was obvious he was proud of how Michael had embraced his journey. They both knew they would be friends for life. Before parting, Blake shared one final philosophy with him. "Guard your thoughts, Michael. Your thoughts become words, your words become actions, your actions become habits, your habits become character, and your character becomes your destiny," the millionaire advised.

Then he turned and began to head toward his yacht, Michael started to choke up. He knew it would be a while before he would have the opportunity to speak with Blake again. He also knew it was time to step to the edge of the cliff, spread his wings and jump. Michael was an eagle, ready to fly. Was he ready to take the next step? Could he do it on his own? He wasn't certain, but he knew he was ready to try.

There was so much he wanted to say to Blake, but he didn't know where to start. Even if he did, there was not nearly enough time to say it all. He still didn't even know why Blake agreed to work with him in the first place.

Although Michael aligned himself with a handful of the leaders in his company, he knew in his heart that Blake Easton, the high school dropout turned multi-millionaire, would always be his mentor. Michael felt the only way he could truly show his appreciation would be by finishing the race he started.

Over the next eighteen months, Michael and Kristen stayed committed to their vision. They strengthened relationships with their up-line leaders and continued to establish bonds with their growing team. They became experts at meeting people and began teaching others techniques like *F.O.R.M.* and *Feel, Felt, Found.* Michael often reflected upon the lessons and techniques he learned from Blake and passed them on to others. He believed the key to success was to under promise and over deliver and he did so every time he brought on a new teammate.

Personal growth became a life mission for the couple. They gave thanks daily for who they were and continued to work towards who they wanted to become. Michael became aware of those who were around him and he constantly asked himself questions like, "Who am I associating with? Where do they have me going? What do they have me thinking?" and most important, "What do they have me becoming?" If he wasn't happy with the answer, he looked for more positive people to spend his time with. That was the main reason why he began spending less time with Billy, Tom and Dean in the first place. He liked them and respected them, but they weren't encouragers. Michael only hoped that Tom wouldn't make the mistake of letting Billy and Dean's negative comments keep him from achieving his own personal goals.

He and Kristen continued to put pictures that represented their dreams on their vision board. Defining a dream was exciting, but what really fired them up was taking pictures off the board each time they had accomplished a goal. Michael also posted several motivational sayings where he would see them daily. Two of his favorites were, '*If you don't create change, change will create you*' and '*people who say it cannot be done should never interrupt people who are doing it.*' While on his path to success, Michael couldn't help but to recognize that the formula for success was really quite simple and could be summarized in two steps. 1. *Get started,* and 2. *Stop stopping.*

As Michael evolved as a person, so did his mission statement.

Michael understood that success was the sum of small efforts repeated day in and day out, so he developed a list of things he would do on a daily basis to grow his business and himself and he posted the list on his bathroom mirror. He called it his daily method of operation and it read as follows.

Things I will do every day:

- Today, I will spend quality time with my family and never lose sight of what is important.
- Today, I will make a new contact and add at least one name to my list because new blood is the lifeblood of my business.
- Today, I will call a new prospect and introduce them to my business because I understand that I will achieve my dreams if I help enough other people achieve their dreams.

- Today, I will follow-through with prospects who have recently looked at my business because I understand that the fortune is in the Follow-up.
- Today, I will encourage my teammates because I believe that people will live up to my expectations of them.
- Today, I will promote our next event because I understand the importance of attending all events and always bringing a freshman class with me.
- Today, I will read from a positive book because I am aware of the fact that I can't give what I don't have and I understand that the problems I have in my life will never be solved by the same thinking that got me there in the first place.
- Today, I will listen to audios on success so I can learn from those who have done what I am trying to do.
- Today, I will lead by example because I am aware that a leader of one may one day become a leader of many, but if I can't lead one I'll never lead any.
- Today, I will give thanks for what I have and what I am becoming because nothing is more honorable than a grateful heart.
- Today, I will eat right, take vitamins and workout because I understand the supreme importance of keeping my body and mind in good health.
- Today, I will do what others *will not* do, so tomorrow I can do what others *cannot* do.

Under the list was a quote from Aristotle that read, "*We are what we repeatedly do; excellence, then, is not an act but a habit.*"

One day, Michael received a call from one of his new teammates. He was a young man who had signed up two weeks earlier. He was struggling after a few friends he had shared the business with laughed at him. As the young man talked openly about his challenges, Michael reflected on when he first reached out to Blake, back when he was on the verge of giving up. He could tell by the semi-defeated tone of the young man's voice that he was in the same place Michael had been just a few years earlier. Michael responded by giving advice on overcoming the word, "*no.*"

"Successful people do what unsuccessful people are not willing to do," Michael said. "Expect some resistance and rejection, that's part of success. You may hear ten no's in a row, but you have to be just as enthusiastic for number eleven. Eventually you'll get yeses and then they'll come frequently. The bottom line is this, unsuccessful people quit before they had a chance to taste success. The key to success is perseverance."

The young man was thankful for Michael's advice. Realizing the importance of association, Michael invited his new teammate to lunch. He wanted to be a positive voice in a world that could often be so negative for a person who is striving for more. After they agreed on a place to meet, Michael reminded the young man that life's problems wouldn't be called "hurdles" if there wasn't a way to get over them.

It was a great moment for Michael who was starting to become a mentor himself. He truly cared more about the newest person earning their first check than he did about himself earning another one. He discovered that when he helped his teammates produce and took his eyes off himself, his income continued to grow and he and Kristen started to achieve significant levels of success within their company. They were experiencing the power of duplication and the type of momentum that could only be developed by someone with an urgency mindset.

Over the next 12 months, each time the couple reached another level or achieved a personal goal, they would call Blake and Laura to share the news. It was one of their favorite things to do because it enabled them to reassure Blake that the time he spent with Michael made a difference.

They continued to build their business and pursue their goals with urgency. They were changing lives. Life was good.

Reunion

FOUR YEARS IN THE business and life for Michael and Kristen was radically different at this point. The business wasn't the only thing growing.

"Don't cry," Michael said, as he stood by Kristen's side, holding her body close to his with one arm. He wasn't sure if he was talking to his wife or to himself as he stood in the school courtyard and waved to their son through the window of his kindergarten classroom.

It was too late. He turned to see tears flowing down Kristen's face. "I can't believe this day is here," she replied.

It wasn't unusual for Kristen to cry at moments like these. She did it when Dylan sat up by himself for the first time, when he learned to crawl and walk, and again when he said his first word. She even did it when his first tooth broke through. Why should his first day at kindergarten be any different? She was sentimental about things like that and Michael wouldn't want it any other way.

Once the last student had entered the building and the school doors closed, he kissed his wife on the cheek and smiled, "Let's go home. He'll be fine."

"Are you sure?" she asked. "He's never been alone."

"He's not alone. He's with a bunch of teachers and other students. He'll be fine," Michael repeated. He looked down at a beautiful little three-year-old girl who was playing with her doll in the school playground, "Come on, Savannah, it's time to go home."

Savannah ran, jumped into Kristen's arms and they began to walk home, through their beautiful neighborhood.

Michael and Kristen were now living in Colts Neck, a prominent community in central New Jersey known for scenic parks, wonderful schools and striking homes. They moved onto a nice cul-de-sac where many young families lived. When they first drove onto the street with their realtor and discovered a group of children riding their bikes, Kristen commented that it looked like a mini-motorcycle gang lived there. Although no one knew who they were, the people who lived on the street waved as their car passed through. Michael and Kristen wanted to give their children a chance to grow up in the type of neighborhood that they used to dream of living in and this community far exceeded their expectations. They were excited for their children.

Savannah was taking a nap and it was quiet in the house. Michael thought this would be a good time to get some work done so he sat down at his computer to review his emails. He opened one from an unknown address and discovered it was from one of his oldest friends, Tom.

Hello Michael,

It's been a long time. I hope this email finds you well. I recently ran into Dean and we thought it would be a great idea to get together for lunch later this week. Let me know if you can make it. I'd love to see you again.

Tom

Long before they moved, Michael had lost touch with his friends Dean, Tom and Billy. They had each taken their own separate journeys and perhaps some would say that destiny had played a role in where they currently were at this stage in their lives. Michael had a different perspective than most. He believed that destiny was a matter of choice, not chance.

Michael was thrilled to receive the message. He immediately sent a reply to Tom and after exchanging several emails, they decided to meet the next day for lunch, at a popular diner on Route 3 in Clifton. Michael logged off the computer and told his wife about the reunion. She was happy that he was going to have a chance to see his old friends. It had been more than four years since the list time they were together.

Tom and Billy were already sitting at a booth in the diner when Michael walked in. He approached, stood near the edge of the booth and looked down at them. Billy was complaining about something insignificant.

"Some things never change," Michael said with a smile.

"Michael!" Tom stood up to hug his friend. "What's up buddy? You look great."

"Thanks, Tom, so do you," he replied, but in reality, he actually thought Tom and Billy looked much older.

Billy quickly scanned Michael's clothing, "Did you mug a GQ model?"

Michael laughed, but he found it to be a peculiar comment given the fact that he wasn't dressed up. He was wearing Khakis and a polo shirt, not exactly a tuxedo, but then it dawned on him that neither Tom nor Billy had ever seen him in anything other than a pair of jeans and a T-shirt. He let the comment pass and began to ask his old friends about how the last four-plus-years had treated them.

Billy was still single and still working in construction, taking on any job he could. He complained that his back and knees have been bothering him, but everything else was the same as when they had last spoke. He also began to complain about how the Rutgers University Football team lost a game they should have won, but Michael just smiled and thought how odd it was that Billy was upset about a team losing a game that didn't mean anything to either of them. His friend never even attended that university. As Michael recalled, even though Billy was offered scholarships to play baseball at several other schools, he never attended *any* university. It was anyone's guess why he wasted so much time and energy worrying about things that had no bearing on his life.

Hearing about Tom's growing family made Michael happy. Tom and his wife now had three children; two boys and a girl—ages seven, four and three. His boys were both into wrestling and his daughter was their biggest cheerleader. Tom's wife, however, was starting a new career because accounting was not enabling them to get ahead the way he had hoped it would. Tom explained that a lot of people were choosing to save money by doing their own taxes.

"Enough about us," Tom said, "Tell us about you. Where have you been?"

Before Michael had a chance to open his mouth, Dean arrived. "Here he is," Michael announced, displaying a vast smile.

"Sorry, I'm late. I was dealing with another problem at work," Dean said, justifying himself.

Dean didn't look the same. He looked worn down and appeared somewhat distracted as he started to make small talk. It was obvious he had other things, like the bank, on his mind. Michael didn't make a big deal of it. He just sat and listened as the others spoke. He couldn't get over the fact that Billy and Tom seemed to be in the exact same place they were four years earlier. Dean, on the other hand, seemed different but Michael couldn't put his finger on it. "So tell me Dean, how's your father?" he asked.

The others were silent. They knew what Michael did not. Dean shrugged his shoulders as if he didn't have a reason for what he was about to say, "They let him go."

"Who let him go?" Michael asked curiously.

"The bank," Dean replied, looking down at his placemat.

"I'm sorry. I didn't know."

"It's okay. He'll find work. It's just difficult to be there every day knowing that I'm working for the people who..." Dean stopped talking.

"Hey, you don't have to explain," Michael said, breaking the silence. "Just tell him I said hello."

"Of course," Dean replied.

Michael's three friends continued to talk, but their voices faded in his mind. He began to think about how much he used to envy Dean and how he almost made the decision not to build his network marketing business because of Dean's negative comments. At that moment, Michael realized for the first time that these three guys had controlled his thinking and kept him at a stalemate for most of his life.

Suddenly, it was clear as day. He wasn't bitter. Instead, he began to feel sorry for them. If only they had understood what he did about network marketing, leveraging, duplication, and personal growth. If only they made the decision to take a chance when he did, because looking back it was so much easier than he thought it was going to be. For several minutes, he tuned out the quiet murmuring of his friends until...

"Michael?" the voice said.

He came out of it and realized all three were looking at him.

"Earth to Michael," Billy laughed.

He refocused, "I'm sorry, what was the question?"

"Tom asked if you're still working at the warehouse," Billy replied.

"Well, no actually."

"Really, last I heard you received a promotion, what happened?" Tom asked.

"Well, that's an interesting question," Michael started, but he wasn't sure if he should go into it. Usually, when someone asks him about what he does for a living, he would answer by saying something like, "I found a way to earn full-time income on a part-time basis," and wait for their curiosity to grow so he could lead the conversation into an appointment. Michael didn't think that was the right thing to say to these three. Perhaps he should just answer with '*the same old things*' and be done with it. He contemplated brushing the whole thing under the carpet, but he knew that wouldn't be the right thing to do. These guys were his friends and they needed to know there was a better way. He breathed in and released.

"Do you remember that business we all looked at several years ago?" He answered.

"What, that pyramid thing?" Billy replied.

Michael smiled, "No, that network marketing thing." he politely corrected.

"Yeah, what about it?" Tom asked.

"I decided to give it a try," he answered.

"And…" Tom prodded, looking for more.

"And, it worked." Michael stated.

"You're telling us that you made money in that thing?" Billy asked, with a slight sense of his signature sarcasm. He did not expect the answer he was about to hear.

"Yes. Kristen retired a couple years ago and I retired last year." Michael countered. The table went silent. "It was a challenge at first, I had to overcome a few things, but once I was over those hurdles, I've been very happy with the results. We've been on a bunch of vacations, moved to Colts Neck, even built a vacation house on a ski slope in Pennsylvania."

"You live in Colts Neck?" Tom remarked, "Are you serious? That's big money."

Michael didn't respond. He didn't feel the need to justify or brag about his results. He knew how happy he and Kristen were. He knew they didn't have the stress in their lives that came with not having enough money. He knew they had strong, unbreakable bonds with teammates throughout the country. He knew he had become a respected leader within the company.

How could he express all that? Instead, he chose to sum it up with one sentence.

"Other than marrying Kristen, it's the best decision I have ever made."

Billy wore a disbelieving expression. Dean's resembled shock. Tom was the first to respond. "But, none of us joined. Who did you do it with?" He asked.

"I started just like everyone else does, alone. A couple of friends and family members eventually signed up, but most of the people I showed early on said no. Luckily, I learned that the word *no* is part of success. I also learned how to meet people and the best way to approach them about the business. I consistently worked on myself. I ended up meeting enough people to build a strong team and a very profitable business, and many of the people that said no early on came back to me and signed up after I started making money."

Billy remained silent. Tom wasn't sure what to say either, but Dean surprised Michael when he muttered, "If anyone could have done it, I knew it would have been you."

Michael privately reminisced about that night in the car several years earlier when Dean tried to talk him out of building the business. He found it ironic that Dean was now acting as if he was supportive. But he kept his thoughts to himself and took the high road. "Listen guys, it worked. I'm speaking from firsthand experience. If you want to take another look at it, I'd be happy to show you how Kristen and I did it."

To his surprise, no one responded to the offer. Instead, they resorted to making small talk over lunch. When the check came thirty minutes later, Michael grabbed it and insisted on paying. Pleasantries were exchanged, and they departed. In the parking lot, they watched as Michael left in a gorgeous sapphire blue Aston Martin.

As he drove past his friends, Michael realized that the night he went to the hotel to see that presentation led to his epic moment. When he decided to pick up the phone and call Blake Easton, everything prior to that moment was preliminary and everything from that moment on was a result of the decision that he made to move his life in another, more positive direction. The outcome of that decision led to rewards that far exceeded his early expectations.

Michael had mixed feelings. He didn't want to see his friends struggle, but he couldn't help but to enjoy the feeling of satisfaction. Not because he was more successful than they were. He had overcome the obstacles that used to beat him, like fear and doubt, and had claimed his victory. He knew that by not quitting he had changed the destiny of his family for generations to come.

Instead of driving straight home, he detoured through Jersey City and stopped in front of the distribution warehouse where he used to work. He wanted to sit there for a few minutes and briefly watch some of his old coworkers as they loaded trucks. The day Michael retired there was no limousine and no trip to New York City. He simply gave his boss his two-week notice and walked out the door on that final day without explanation. Michael wasn't sure why he felt compelled to stop by his old place of employment. Perhaps it was his way of closing that chapter of his life. He was about to drive off when his cell phone rang.

"Hello, this is Michael."

"Michael. It's Tom."

Surprised, "Hi Tom, What's up?"

"I just have to ask you one question." His friend began, "Is this for real?"

Even over the phone, Michael could hear the stress in Tom's voice. He had become great at reading people and he could tell this required more than a yes or no answer. "Tom, I never knew life could be so rewarding."

"I'm broke," his voice cracked, "I mean, really broke. I don't have enough money to buy my kids new clothes. I don't know what to do. Can you help me?"

"Tom, you're my oldest and best friend. I'd be honored to help you. If you are teachable, willing to work and do what I tell you to do, one year from now you will never again have to say the words *I don't have the money*." Michael assured. "Where are you right now?"

"I'm home."

"I'll be there in twenty minutes."

"You'll come over now?"

"Of course I will. You asked me for help. Is your wife available? I'd like her to be there so I can talk with the both of you together. If I'm going to help you I want the two of you to be on the same page."

"She'll be here," Tom assured.

Michael met with the couple and shared his business plan with them. They agreed to let him teach them what they needed to do to get their family out of debt and on the path to financial success. When he returned home, Michael told Kristen about what happened. Her heart went out to Tom. She knew it must have been hard to make that call, but then she remembered what her husband went through years ago when he called Blake. It was coming full circle. She was proud of Michael for everything he had done, and for persevering. She didn't assume he knew this, she told him.

The Ripple Effect

THE CONVENTION HALL in the Orlando World Center was buzzing. More than five thousand people were anticipating the speech of the next couple who were about to take the stage. The lights went down. A photomontage set to music began to play on the big screen. The first slide featured two side-by-side baby photos. They were pictures of the couple when they were infants. The pictures that followed documented key moments in each of their lives. They were two average kids with dreams. Two kids who met, fell in love, and struggled to find their way through the challenges of life. As the video progressed, it became clear that those two innocent kids have achieved success. In fact, they were moments away from being recognized for achieving their company's highest level.

When the song ended, the lights came up and Michael and Kristen were standing in the center of the stage with their children. There was a thunderous applause, the kind that could only be given to honor people who have overcome great challenges and helped many others do the same. They had been working for this moment. The couple was dressed in formal attire. Michael wore an expensive dark gray double-breasted suit. Kristen wore a beautiful full-length dress. Their children, although young, were equally as striking in dress and poise.

Kristen introduced Dylan and Savannah to the crowd of people, whom they referred to as their extended family. She spoke for a few minutes and thanked their team for joining them on this journey and for being people who fought for their dreams. She then thanked her husband for being an example for her children and a leader for so many others. She told him how much she loved him for stretching so far out of his comfort zone and building this business for their family and for generations of family to come. It was an emotional moment for the couple.

After a loving embrace, Kristen and the kids stepped backstage so Michael could address the crowd. By now, he was a seasoned speaker. He began by sharing their struggles and encouraging everyone to embrace the challenges they were facing in their own lives. He assured them that the process they will go through by overcoming those challenges and struggles would shape them into the people they are destined to become. He spoke to them about how easy it is to succumb to cynicism and how important it is for individuals to accept responsibility for their own actions.

"Most people will never experience greatness because they are not willing to pay the price and because the vehicle they've chosen does not provide them with the opportunity to positively impact the lives of others," Michael began. "Most jobs will never give you the satisfaction of bringing a spouse home from work so you can raise your own children. Most opportunities don't encourage personal growth or offer you a chance to develop skills that can enhance all aspects of your life. Most vehicles do not offer a way to generate time and financial freedom as well as the opportunity to create a legacy, but the one you have your hands on does! This vehicle offers all that and much more. So my question to you is this... Why are you here?"

The crowd was silent. They were hanging on his every word. He repeated the question, "Why are you here? What do you stand for? What is your life's purpose? What made you get on a plane, or drive halfway across the country in your car to come here this weekend? What are you doing this for? If you can answer that question... you're halfway there."

Michael stepped away from the podium and closer to the audience. He could see the first few rows, but the massive stage lights prevented him from seeing beyond that. He didn't need to see them, he knew they were there and he knew they were listening. "This business is not for people who need it—there are millions of people who *need* it. This business is for people who *want* it!" he stressed. "It's for people who are sick and tired of being sick and tired, like I used to be."

Michael then spoke about the rewards that his family had received by finishing what they started. He talked about his ski home in the mountains and about their new dream home in Colts Neck. Michael wasn't trying to impress anyone. He was trying to impress upon them the importance of going after their dreams. It wasn't the vacations and the cars and the material things that he stressed. It was what each and every one in the audience would become by finishing the race. "Only a person who is chasing a dream is living a life of purpose," he explained.

It was also about the thrill of teaming up with a partner, in his case his wife, and accomplishing goals that once seemed impossible. He gave Kristen the credit for their success because he knew he couldn't have done it without her unconditional support. During his talk, he explained to the audience that they should continue to make their living from nine to five, but begin to work on their fortune before nine and after five.

Michael's message was coming across loud and clear. The audience felt his passion and sincerity. He warned about critics and in a commanding voice shouted, "People who say it cannot be done should never interrupt people who are doing it!" The crowd rose to their feet, and produced a thunderous cheer and applause.

Michael signaled for them to settle down. Near the foot of the podium was a clock that was counting down. He had a few minutes left, which wasn't much time. "I need to say something," he said, as he motioned for them to sit back in their seats. "It's about someone important."

The crowd began to hush each other until it was once again silent. Michael continued, "When you throw a pebble into the ocean, the pebble disappears. What most don't realize is that the ripple that pebble produces will travel for more than a hundred miles. The same effect occurs with people. The life you touch may only be one, but that one may go on and affect hundreds, even thousands more."

He took a moment to compose himself. Looking out into the audience, he located Blake and Laura Easton in the third row. Michael knew the biggest reason why he was on that stage was Blake Easton's guidance.

"To my friend, Blake and his wife Laura, you have blessed our family with your friendship and support. Blake, I will always consider you more than a friend. You are my mentor and an example of what I strive to become. If I can change one person's life, the way you have changed mine, I will consider my time on this earth a success. In your honor, I would like to share a quote from Mark Twain with the thousands of friends in the room with us tonight. Twain said, *'Twenty years from now you will be more disappointed by the things that you didn't do than by the ones you did. So throw off the bowlines. Sail away from the safe harbor. Catch the trade winds in your sail. Explore. Dream. Discover'...* and in the words of my friend Blake Easton, *You can't discover new worlds unless you leave the port of familiar shores.*"

Blake and Laura were moved by the talk. Michael then looked down in the front row at Tom and his wife who were attending their first conference. Once he and Tom connected eyes, he continued, "Life is meant to be a wonderful journey, but only those who dream big enough and fight hard enough will ever come to that realization."

He concluded his speech with a call to action for everyone in attendance. "Decide what impact you want to have, what difference you want to make and how you want others to remember you. Do it now, before it's too late. We only have so much time on this earth to make our mark. Today is the day to start your legacy. Today is the day to begin living the way you know you were meant to live. Yesterday is gone and tomorrow never comes, all you have is today."

As he ended his speech, the crowd gave him a standing ovation. It was clear from the response of the crowd that Michael had moved beyond success to significance. His words were changing lives.

Backstage, Kristen approached and embraced her husband. She was proud and he was grateful. They held each other tight for a moment. When they released, the couple noticed Blake Easton emerging from the darkness. As he came closer, Michael could see the reflection of tears in the mentor's eyes. The two men stood face to face for an instant before Michael realized his friend had something important to share.

"Blake? What is it?"

"I've been wrestling with something since the day I received your call. Laura kept urging me to tell you, but I couldn't. When you spoke of the ripple effect, I knew that was a sign for me."

Michael was puzzled, but attentive. He stood silent waiting for Blake to continue.

"You know I dropped out of high school after my father passed away and I shared how desperate of a time that was for me," the mentor reiterated as his eyes, which were lowered toward the floor, continued to well up.

"Yes," Michael replied. He wasn't sure how to react, so he remained still.

"About a week after I dropped out, I was sitting on a tree stump in a junkyard looking at a pile of garbage, feeling like I was no more valuable than anything in it," Blake's voice broke as he shared, "It was the weakest moment of my life. I was a complete failure. I knew I wasn't going to amount to anything and I couldn't think of any reason to go on. That was the day I decided to…"

After a long silence Michael broke the awkward moment, "Decided to what?"

"To end my life," the mentor said. He raised his watery eyes to meet Michael's, whose eyes had also welled up. Blake continued, "I just finished writing a note to my mother. That day in the junkyard, I was contemplating how I was going to do it. I didn't have any answers, I only knew the decision was made, but then I heard footsteps behind me. I turned to see a boy who I vaguely knew approaching. His name was Tim Harper."

Kristen squeezed his arm tightly as chills ran down Michael's spine. "My father?"

"Yes. He was cutting through the yard on his way home from school, but he saw me and to my surprise, he stopped to talk." Blake took a moment to gather his composure. "Your father introduced himself and said he was sorry to hear about my loss. I thanked him, but I just wanted him to leave so I could get on with it, but you know how stubborn your father was," Blake half-chuckled. Michael tried, but couldn't manage a smile, the mentor continued, "He said something to me that day, Michael, something that changed the direction of my life."

"What… what did my father say?" he asked.

"He told me that he admired my strength. He said it took a lot of courage to drop out to take care of my mother and that he wished he was as strong as I was. He said that if there was anything I needed not to hesitate to ask him."

Tears welled in Michael's eyes.

"Michael, when your father told me he admired my strength I felt ashamed. At that moment, I vowed never to give up. The words he said to me that day would mean nothing to most people, but they meant everything to me. The pebble your father threw into the ocean that day changed my life," the mentor said.

"And you changed mine," Michael grasped.

"And you are changing the lives of thousands of others," Blake said. "Laura was right. You needed to know."

Laura appeared and placed her arm around Kristen. The four of them embraced.

"Thank you," Michael said. He was unable to hold back the tears. "Thank you for telling me."

In an unexpected way, this news came as a relief to Michael. He knew that his father's small act of kindness and generous words made an enormous difference not just in Blake's life, but in his own. He made a pledge to always speak kind words to others because he could never know what personal challenges people were going through. This was easy for the man who had learned to take his eyes off himself and place them on others—a lesson he learned from his mentor.

"Michael, Kristen," a voice called.

All four turned to see a man franticly waving the couple back onto the stage. Michael thought something was wrong. He wore the look of concern.

"Hurry," the man said.

"What happened?" Michael asked.

"You're names were called. You just won the Eagle award!"

Blake, who still had his hand on Michael's upper arm, squeezed tightly when he heard the news. They looked at each other. Words were not necessary.

"Go on you two," Blake said proudly, "Go accept your award."

Michael and Kristen embraced. They worked so hard to achieve this goal, but they did not know they achieved it until this very moment. The couple grasped hands and hurried back to the stage.

The Perfect Day

IT WAS JULY THIRTEENTH. Michael and Kristen sat on the beach in Martinique, their hips touching, as they overlooked the beautiful island landscape. The ocean was calm and blue. The half-full glass of lemonade in Michael's hand was sweating. He glanced down at his Rolex. It was 3:21 pm. He looked over at his children who were playing in the sand near the ocean with beach buckets. Grabbing a plastic shovel from their beach bag, he lifted himself from the blanket, walked over, sat on the sand near the kids and asked, "Who wants to make a sand castle?"

Enthusiastically, both Dylan and Savannah replied, "I do!"

Kristen smiled. Michael looked over at his beautiful wife, winked, and began digging. No stress, no deadlines, and no uncertainty to their future... just time with the people who mattered the most. Life was great.

"Finished," Michael said.

With three-tiers and robust columns, the sandcastle was a thing of beauty—a masterpiece.

"It's awesome, Dad," Dylan shouted.

"Take a picture of it, Mom," Savannah insisted.

Michael agreed. He grabbed the clothing bag to retrieve the camera when something down the beach captured his attention. "You've got to be kidding me," he said in strong tone.

Kristen immediately whipped her head around, "What is it?"

Michael just stared, frozen like a statue, looking down the beach toward the crashing waves.

Kristen followed Michael's gaze, which was fixed on a small group of people. Children were running back forth, playing in the water as the waves leveled upon the shore. A volleyball game was in progress. Kristen couldn't pinpoint what had Michael's attention.

"It can't be," Michael said. For a brief second, Savannah and Dylan lost interest in the magnificent sandcastle and turned in the direction their father was looking.

"Is that Jerry?" Michael said.

Jerry was Billy's younger brother, one of the three friends with whom Michael grew up. Michael wondered what Jerry was doing on Martinique Island and what a coincident it was. *I haven't seen him since he played little league,* he thought.

"What's he doing here?" Kristen asked.

"I'm about to find out," Michael said as he got up, brushed the sand from his knees and started to walk in Jerry's direction. Jerry and a few guys were watching and cheering a beach volleyball game in progress. As he approached, Michael pondered the past. It had been years since he had last seen Jerry. He wasn't even 100% sure it was Jerry, although his assuredness grew with every step. *Jerry Caruso... a spitting image of your brother Billy... what are you doing way down here?*

"Excuse me," Michael said awkwardly. Jerry and his friends turned around as he made his appeal, "Jerry Caruso?"

"That depends upon who's asking." Jerry replied. Jerry's friends busted out laughing as Jerry stood broad-shouldered, like he was ready to enter a street fight.

Michael held out his hand in gesture, "Michael Harper."

Jerry stood for a moment, unsure, and then it registered. "You gotta be kidding me," Jerry said as a smile appeared. He reached out, grabbed Michael's hand as if to shake it, and then jerked Michael in for a manly bear hug that nearly took his breath away.

"What are you doing here?" Michael asked.

"I was just gonna ask you the same thing," Jerry responded.

Jerry's posture and physique was similar to "a younger version" Billy, only he was a bit more muscular and his tight shirt reinforced his macho weight-lifter look.

Michael turned and pointed to Kristen, Dylan and Savannah. "I'm on vacation with my wife and kids. We have a condo here."

Jerry looked past Michael in the direction he was pointing and made eye contact with Kristen. She waved. Jerry waved back.

Jerry turned to Barry, his best friend, and smacked him on the chest to get his full attention, "Check it out... this is the guy who went to high school with my brother, Billy." His friends nodded and smiled but they didn't have a clue who Michael was. "You know..." Jerry continued, "Millionaire Mike." Jerry's friends took a second look and they responded as if they had just met a famous movie star.

"No way," said Ken. Ken was Barry's twin brother. They both played on Jerry's little league team.

"You're *the* millionaire Dean told us about?" Craig said. Craig was Dean's younger cousin. Craig's dad worked in a bank downtown and was on the same bowling team as Dean's dad.

"That's him," Jerry said with a big smile.

Michael stood there—a bit shocked at their reaction. Trying to take the focus off him, he spoke up, "So, you didn't tell me, what you're doing here?"

"I was caller number FIVE," Jerry said.

Craig stepped forward, pointing his thumb toward Jerry, "Luckiest guy you'll ever meet."

Michael tried not to laugh, but he couldn't help but notice the shade variation from Craig's tan lines across his biceps, exposing his white shoulders and chest. Michael remembered Craig because he had red hair and freckles. His nickname was "Red." He was the catcher on Jerry's little league team and every time there was a foul ball, Craig would throw his catcher's mask, revealing the neon red hair, and the home crowd would chant, "Red... Red... Red!"

"Get out of here," Jerry replied as he pushed Red back. "I'm not lucky. Do you even know how many times I've called that stupid radio station over the past three months, trying to win something? I called day and night—nothing else to do."

"What do you do?" Michael asked Jerry.

"Currently... I collect unemployment, but I was working with Billy in construction until the recession hit."

"Yeah, but just think of it this way, if you still had a job, we wouldn't be here—now, would we?" Red said.

"Are you guys next?" a young girl shouted out from the other side of the volleyball net. Jerry and his friends had been waiting for their turn to play. The previous game just ended and they had next game.

"C'mon Jerry, we're up," Barry said.

Like a group of marines preparing to invade a hostile territory, the friends were ready for war. "Let's do this!" Red shouted.

"You guys go on without me. I'm gonna go catch up with Millionaire Mike," Jerry said.

"C'mon dude, it's a four-man team," Red said.

"I'll take his place."

The guys turned and looked. It was the young girl, now standing close enough to hear their conversation. Her hair was braided with strands on each side. She was apparently on the losing team, but was anxious to play again and Jerry's bail out was her perfect opportunity.

"Sure," Ken responded as he sized her up, "I saw you spike the ball, you're better than Jerry." The others laughed. Ken turned to Jerry, "We'll catch up with you later." Without hesitation, Ken, Red, Barry and the young girl took their assumed positions on the volleyball court.

Jerry and Michael walked back to where Kristen, Dylan and Savannah were. The kids were still adding onto the sand castle. Michael introduced his friend to his family. Then, Jerry and Michael made their way to a nearby Tiki Hut on the beach and sat on stools at the counter.

"Can I get you guys something to drink?" a server asked as he placed two napkins down on the counter, one if front of Michael and one in front of Jerry.

"Lemonade," Michael said.

"I'll have the same," Jerry said.

The server returned and placed their drinks on the napkin. The tall glasses, full of ice cubes and lemon wedges were decorated with an umbrella and a bright red straw that protruded out of the ice.

Jerry filled Michael in on the last twelve years of his life. Jerry, like his brother Billy, excelled at sports. Unlike Billy, however, Jerry possessed a high level of drive and determination, which greatly complimented his athletic ability. In his senior year of high school, he led his baseball team to the state championship. His performance that year made him one of the top recruits in the country. He obtained a full scholarship to Florida State University and helped the Seminoles win their division and make an appearance in the College World Series. Attempting to catch a foul ball in the second inning of their first game, Jerry injured his shoulder and was sidelined for the remainder of the game. Stanford went on to win that game 16-5 and two days later, Miami beat the Seminoles 7-5, eliminating them from the competition.

The following year, Jerry, Ken, Barry and Red were reunited. Oddly, all four friends were drafted at the same time by the Florida Marlins and played for their farm team in Miami. Even though it was only the Minors, very few ever made it to this level. The fact that they knew each other from as far back as their little league days made the story much more interesting. Local papers loved writing about "the fab four." It was supposed to be the most exciting time of his life, but Jerry's shoulder injury continued to plague him and affect his hitting. His batting average dropped in his first season and he was cut from the team the following year during spring training. His baseball career ended and he returned home. Out of options, Jerry was forced to take a construction job with Billy. That lasted only four months. Due to the economic slowdown, home construction tanked and Jerry was let go.

Michael was moved by Jerry's story. His determination to win, compete, and persevere was captivating. Needless to say, however, being unemployed and out of work took its toll on Jerry's self-esteem. Although he had been through rough times, Michael saw incredible potential in his embattled friend. Perhaps Jerry just needed someone to believe in him again.

By now, Kristen, Dylan and Savannah had already headed back to the condominium and Jerry's friends were nowhere in sight.

Jerry took the straw and stirred his lemonade. "I was hoping this trip would clear my mind and maybe help me find myself," Jerry sighed and gave a half smile, "sounds funny, find myself... at my age." After a moment of reflection, he continued, "Anyway, reuniting with my pals and old teammates hasn't helped. Sure, we're having a blast, but they are only here for three days. They fly back to Miami tomorrow for a home game against the Cubs." Jerry lowered his head in defeat, thinking about how he missed baseball more than ever—it was his life.

Getting a grip on his emotions, Jerry perked up, "But, I have the condo to myself for two more days, then it's back to Jersey." Jerry paused for a moment, took a sip and said, "Hanging with the guys just makes me regret trying to make it to the big leagues. I feel like I'm reliving my past."

"You know, a rearview mirror is smaller than a windshield for a reason. If you let your past experiences get in the way of the present, you'll end up losing your future," Michael said.

"That's easy for you to say... you're rich," Jerry replied.

Michael laughed. "Money doesn't have anything to do with it." Michael retrieved a lemon from his drink, moved his glass aside and squeezed the wedge, causing the juice to drop on his napkin.

"Is this where you say, 'If someone gives you a lemon, make lemonade?'" Jerry said.

"No, but I like that saying," Michael replied. "If I squeeze this lemon, I can make lemonade. But if that's all I use this lemon for, it will only serve a temporary purpose. Once the juice is gone, the lemon seems to lose its value and is quickly discarded in the trash. But what's left in the lemon?"

"I don't know."

"Seeds," Michael said. "Listen, Jerry, anyone can cut a lemon and count how many seeds are in it, but no one can tell you how many lemons will come from one good seed. Don't focus on the lemon. Instead, focus on what will become of the seed."

Just then, Michael's cell phone rang. "Hi Honey." It was Kristen letting Michael know that the kids were hungry and to see if he wanted to join them for an early dinner. "Sure, I'll be right there."

"I'm sorry. I'm keeping you from your family," Jerry said.

"Not a problem," Michael replied.

Michael slid his cell phone back into his pocket and then took out his wallet.

"Here's my card."

Jerry looked at it. It read, "*Michael Harper, Entrepreneur*." Jerry flipped the card over and saw Michael's cell phone number.

"I've been where you are Jerry. I understand your situation better than you can imagine. I want you to call me if you need anything."

Jerry held Michael's business card in his hand and just stared at it. "Wow," he said.

Michael stood up and placed his hand on Jerry's shoulder, "I mean it Jerry... call me. Call me anytime."

Jerry turned and looked Michael straight in the eye. For a moment, Michael thought Jerry was going to break down and cry. "Take care, Jerry," Michael said.

As he walked toward the condo, Michael couldn't help but remember when he met Blake at his Dad's funeral. He replayed Jerry's story in his mind and likened it to his own. He remembered how he felt hopeless working at his old job, living paycheck to paycheck. Back then, everything seemed so much more difficult. He hoped Jerry wouldn't let his current circumstances keep him from pursuing the life he deserved to live. Just then, Michael's cell rang. He thought it was Kristen again. He looked at his phone, but didn't recognize the number.

"Hello, this is Michael."

"You said to call anytime..."